THE ULTIMATE
EIGHTH GRADE
MATH WORKBOOK

ISBN: 9781947569638
28 27 26 25 24 3 4 5 6 7
Printed in the USA

Table of Contents

Learn!

Taking the **square root** of a number is the opposite of squaring a number. The symbol $\sqrt{}$ is called a **radical sign**, and it tells you to find the positive square root. A **perfect square** is a number with integer square roots.

Try it! Evaluate $\sqrt{16}$. Find the positive number that is equal to 16 when it is squared.

You know that $4^2 = 4 \times 4 = 16$. So, $\sqrt{16} = 4$. The number 16 is a perfect square because it has an integer square root.

Evaluate each expression.

$\sqrt{25} = \underline{\ \ 5\ \ }$ $\sqrt{9} = \underline{\hspace{2cm}}$ $\sqrt{4} = \underline{\hspace{2cm}}$

$\sqrt{1} = \underline{\hspace{2cm}}$ $\sqrt{64} = \underline{\hspace{2cm}}$ $\sqrt{49} = \underline{\hspace{2cm}}$

$\sqrt{100} = \underline{\hspace{2cm}}$ $\sqrt{81} = \underline{\hspace{2cm}}$ $\sqrt{36} = \underline{\hspace{2cm}}$

$\sqrt{144} = \underline{\hspace{2cm}}$ $\sqrt{225} = \underline{\hspace{2cm}}$ $\sqrt{169} = \underline{\hspace{2cm}}$

$\sqrt{196} = \underline{\hspace{2cm}}$ $\sqrt{400} = \underline{\hspace{2cm}}$ $\sqrt{324} = \underline{\hspace{2cm}}$

IXL.com
skill ID

9RS

For more practice, visit IXL.com or the IXL mobile app and enter this code in the search bar.

Learn!

You may see radical signs with symbols in front of them. Look below to find out how to evaluate these types of expressions.

$-\sqrt{16} = -4$ A negative sign in front of the radical tells you to find the opposite of the positive square root.

$\pm\sqrt{16} = \pm4$ A plus-minus sign, $\pm$, in front of the radical tells you to find both the positive square root and the opposite of the positive square root. So, $\pm\sqrt{16}$ is 4 or –4, which you can write as ±4.

Evaluate each expression.

$-\sqrt{49} = $ _____

$\sqrt{121} = $ _____

$\pm\sqrt{4} = $ _____

$\pm\sqrt{400} = $ _____

$-\sqrt{256} = $ _____

$-\sqrt{144} = $ _____

$\sqrt{289} = $ _____

$-\sqrt{81} = $ _____

$\pm\sqrt{361} = $ _____

$\pm\sqrt{324} = $ _____

$\sqrt{400} = $ _____

$\pm\sqrt{225} = $ _____

Learn!

Taking the square root of a number is the opposite, or inverse, of squaring a number. You can use these inverse operations to solve equations.

Try it! Solve $x^2 = 25$.

$x^2 = 25$ Take the square root of both sides of the equation.

$x = \pm 5$ Since $5^2 = 25$ and $(-5)^2 = 25$, both $x = 5$ and $x = -5$ are possible solutions. So, you can write your answer as $x = \pm 5$.

Solve each equation for the variable.

$a^2 = 16$ $w^2 = 121$ $m^2 = 36$

$y^2 = 100$ $z^2 = 49$ $k^2 = 225$

$c^2 = 169$ $p^2 = 256$ $b^2 = 196$

$s^2 = \dfrac{16}{49}$ $n^2 = \dfrac{25}{144}$ $g^2 = \dfrac{9}{400}$

$j^2 = 289$ $t^2 = \dfrac{64}{361}$

IXL.com
skill ID
NNA

Cube roots of perfect cubes

Learn!

Taking the **cube root** of a number is the opposite of cubing a number. The symbol $\sqrt[3]{\ }$ tells you to find the cube root. A **perfect cube** is a number with an integer cube root.

Try it! Evaluate $\sqrt[3]{27}$. Find the number that is equal to 27 when it is cubed.

You know that $3^3 = 3 \times 3 \times 3 = 27$. So, $\sqrt[3]{27} = 3$. The number 27 is a perfect cube because it has an integer cube root.

Evaluate each expression.

$\sqrt[3]{8} = \underline{\ 2\ }$ $\sqrt[3]{125} = \underline{\quad}$ $\sqrt[3]{64} = \underline{\quad}$

$\sqrt[3]{343} = \underline{\quad}$ $\sqrt[3]{1} = \underline{\quad}$ $\sqrt[3]{729} = \underline{\quad}$

$\sqrt[3]{1,000} = \underline{\quad}$ $\sqrt[3]{216} = \underline{\quad}$ $\sqrt[3]{512} = \underline{\quad}$

$\sqrt[3]{27,000} = \underline{\quad}$ $\sqrt[3]{8,000} = \underline{\quad}$ $\sqrt[3]{1,331} = \underline{\quad}$

$\sqrt[3]{64,000} = \underline{\quad}$ $\sqrt[3]{1,728} = \underline{\quad}$

IXL.com
skill ID
RYG

Learn!

You can also take cube roots of negative numbers.

Try it! Evaluate $\sqrt[3]{-27}$. Find the number that is equal to −27 when it is cubed.

You know that $(-3)^3 = (-3) \times (-3) \times (-3) = -27$. So, $\sqrt[3]{-27} = -3$.

Evaluate each expression.

$\sqrt[3]{-8}$ = _____

$\sqrt[3]{1,000}$ = _____

$\sqrt[3]{-512}$ = _____

$\sqrt[3]{64}$ = _____

$\sqrt[3]{216}$ = _____

$\sqrt[3]{-729}$ = _____

$-\sqrt[3]{27,000}$ = _____

$\sqrt[3]{-\dfrac{27}{125}}$ = _____

$-\sqrt[3]{216,000}$ = _____

$\sqrt[3]{125,000}$ = _____

$\sqrt[3]{\dfrac{1,331}{1,728}}$ = _____

$\sqrt[3]{-343,000}$ = _____

KEEP IT
GOING!

Evaluate $-\sqrt[3]{-8}$. Then, compare that value to your first answer above. How did your answer change?

Solving equations with cube roots

Learn!

Taking the cube root is the inverse of cubing a number. You can use these inverse operations to solve equations.

Try it! Solve $x^3 = 64$.

$x^3 = 64$ Take the cube root of both sides of the equation.

$x = 4$ Since $4^3 = 64$, $x = 4$.

Solve each equation for the variable.

$z^3 = 64$

$b^3 = -1$

$d^3 = 343$

$j^3 = 1{,}728$

$p^3 = -1{,}331$

$t^3 = 125$

$w^3 = 27{,}000$

$m^3 = \dfrac{1}{343}$

$s^3 = -216{,}000$

$a^3 = -\dfrac{27}{512}$

$y^3 = -512{,}000$

$f^3 = -\dfrac{729}{1{,}000}$

$q^3 = \dfrac{64}{1{,}331}$

$r^3 = -1{,}000{,}000$

IXL.com
skill ID
TQ5

Solve each equation using square or cube roots. Use your answers to draw a path from start to finish.

START

| $x^2 = 64$ | ±4 | $x^3 = 125$ | –5 | $x^2 = 49$ | ±7 | $x^2 = 289$ |

| –16 | ±8 | 15 | 5 | ±9 | ±17 | 17 |

| $x^3 = -27$ | 3 | $x^2 = 169$ | ±13 | $x^2 = \dfrac{4}{121}$ | $\pm\dfrac{2}{11}$ | $x^3 = 1{,}331$ |

| –9 | 3 | ±12 | 7 | $\pm\dfrac{8}{12}$ | 11 | 13 |

| $x^3 = \dfrac{8}{125}$ | $\dfrac{2}{5}$ | $x^3 = -343$ | ± 20 | $x^2 = 400$ | 16 | $x^3 = -1{,}000$ |

| $\dfrac{4}{5}$ | $-\dfrac{2}{5}$ | 7 | –7 | ±2 | –10 | 10 |

| $x^2 = 225$ | ±15 | $x^3 = -\dfrac{512}{729}$ | $-\dfrac{8}{9}$ | $x^2 = \dfrac{25}{36}$ | $\pm\dfrac{5}{6}$ | **FINISH** |

Challenge!

IXL.com
Checkpoint ID
UF5

You can write any rational number as a decimal using long division. Remember that the decimal form of a rational number will either terminate or repeat.

Try it! Write each rational number as a decimal using long division. Write repeating decimals with a bar over any digits that repeat.

$\frac{2}{5} = $ __0.4__

$$\begin{array}{r} 0.4 \\ 5\overline{)2.0} \\ -\ 0 \\ \hline 2\ 0 \\ -\ 2\ 0 \\ \hline 0 \end{array}$$

$\frac{3}{8} = $ _____

$-\frac{1}{6} = $ _____

$\frac{2}{11} = $ _____

$-\frac{43}{20} = $ _____

$-\frac{16}{9} = $ _____

$\frac{19}{4} = $ _____

$4\frac{5}{12} = $ _____

$-\frac{7}{3} = $ _____

$-1\frac{42}{80} = $ _____

IXL.com
skill ID
M2D

Match each rational number to its equivalent decimal.

$-\dfrac{23}{8}$	$2.0\overline{45}$
$\dfrac{1}{55}$	$5.\overline{1}$
$-\dfrac{81}{16}$	4.15
$-\dfrac{9}{40}$	-2.875
$\dfrac{14}{15}$	-0.225
$\dfrac{46}{9}$	-0.72
$\dfrac{83}{20}$	$0.0\overline{18}$
$-\dfrac{18}{25}$	$-5.\overline{6}$
$\dfrac{45}{22}$	-5.0625
$-\dfrac{17}{3}$	$0.9\overline{3}$

Learn!

As an added challenge, you may want to go the other way and write a repeating decimal as a fraction. Try it! Write $0.\overline{2}$ as a fraction by following the steps below.

$$x = 0.\overline{2}$$

First, set the repeating decimal equal to x.

$$x \cdot 10^1 = 0.\overline{2} \cdot 10^1$$
$$10x = 2.\overline{2}$$

Then, multiply both sides by 10^n, where n is the number of digits that repeat in the decimal. Here, 1 digit repeats in $0.\overline{2}$, so $n = 1$. Then simplify both sides of the equation.

$$10x - x = 2.\overline{2} - 0.\overline{2}$$
$$9x = 2$$

Next, subtract the original repeating decimal from both sides of the equation. Since $x = 0.\overline{2}$, you can subtract x from $10x$ on the left side of the equation and $0.\overline{2}$ from $2.\overline{2}$ on the right side.

$$\frac{9x}{9} = \frac{2}{9}$$

Then, simplify.

$$x = \frac{2}{9}$$

Last, solve for x, and simplify if needed.

Write each repeating decimal as a proper fraction or mixed number.

$0.\overline{09} = \underline{\frac{1}{11}}$ $0.\overline{7} = \underline{\qquad}$ $0.\overline{36} = \underline{\qquad}$

$$x = 0.\overline{09}$$
$$x \cdot 10^2 = 0.\overline{09} \cdot 10^2$$
$$100x = 9.\overline{09}$$
$$100x - x = 9.\overline{09} - 0.\overline{09}$$
$$99x = 9$$
$$\frac{99x}{99} = \frac{9}{99}$$
$$x = \frac{1}{11}$$

Learn!

In some repeating decimals, some of the digits do not repeat. You can write these decimals as fractions by following the steps below. Try it for $0.7\overline{8}$.

$$x = 0.7\overline{8}$$

First, set the repeating decimal equal to x.

$$x \cdot 10^1 = 0.7\overline{8} \cdot 10^1$$
$$10x = 7.\overline{8}$$

Then, multiply both sides of the equation by the appropriate power of ten and simplify.

$$10x - x = 7.\overline{8} - 0.7\overline{8}$$
$$9x = 7.1$$

Next, subtract x from one side and the repeating decimal from the other. Then, simplify. To find $7.\overline{8} - 0.7\overline{8}$, notice that all of the repeating 8s beyond the tenths place cancel out. So, find $7.8 - 0.7$, which is 7.1.

$$\frac{9x}{9} = \frac{7.1}{9}$$

Last, solve for x, writing both the numerator and denominator as integers. Simplify if needed.

$$x = \frac{71}{90}$$

Write each repeating decimal as a proper fraction or mixed number.

$0.2\overline{6} = $ _____

$0.0\overline{8} = $ _____

$1.\overline{5} = $ _____

Learn!

Real numbers are made up of rational numbers and **irrational numbers**. Some rational numbers can be classified further. The diagrams below show different types of real numbers.

Rational numbers can be written as fractions. When written as decimals, they either terminate or repeat.

$$0.\overline{18} \qquad 1\frac{3}{4} \qquad -4.278$$

Integers are counting numbers, their opposites, and zero.

$$-31 \qquad -4 \qquad -100$$

Whole numbers are counting numbers and zero.

Natural numbers are counting numbers.

$$1, 2, 3, 4 \ldots$$

Irrational numbers cannot be written as a fraction. When written as decimals, they go on forever without repeating. Square roots of non-perfect squares and cube roots of non-perfect cubes are irrational.

$$\pi \qquad \sqrt{2} \qquad -\sqrt[3]{11}$$

Write the most specific classification for each number. Remember to first simplify fractions, square roots, or cube roots, if possible.

832 _____natural number_____

0 _____

$\sqrt{16}$ _____

$-\dfrac{10}{2}$ _____

$\sqrt[3]{4}$ _____

−74 _____

$\sqrt{3}$ _____

−π _____

−99.3 _____

IXL.com
skill ID
VR7

Find the path from start to finish. Your path should go only through spaces with a rational number. No diagonal moves are allowed.

START ↓

$\dfrac{5}{6}$	-35	$-\sqrt{11}$	-51.8
π	$\sqrt{100}$	$\sqrt[3]{6}$	$10.\overline{24}$
$-8.\overline{6}$	0.125	$\sqrt{42}$	$150{,}326$
0	$-\sqrt{20}$	$-\sqrt{2}$	$\sqrt[3]{64}$
$-\dfrac{1}{4}$	$\dfrac{10}{2}$	$-\pi$	$\sqrt{3}$
4π	$\sqrt{25} - 99.\overline{7}$	$-\sqrt{36} + \sqrt{1}$	$3\dfrac{2}{11}$
$\dfrac{77}{\sqrt[3]{343}}$	$-\sqrt[3]{5}$	$-\sqrt[3]{4}$	$-4.\overline{8}$
312.5	$-\dfrac{16}{3} + \pi$	$\sqrt{5}$	0.3

FINISH

IXL.com
skill ID
NV6

Learn!

If a whole number is not a perfect square, its square root is irrational. You can approximate the number's square root by finding the two numbers that the square root falls between.

Try it! Approximate $\sqrt{29}$ by finding the two whole numbers that it falls between.

$25 < 29 < 36$ — First, find the two nearest perfect squares. The perfect square just below 29 is 25. The perfect square just above 29 is 36.

$\sqrt{25} < \sqrt{29} < \sqrt{36}$ — Then, find the square root of the two nearest perfect squares.

$5 < \sqrt{29} < 6$ — Since $\sqrt{25} = 5$ and $\sqrt{36} = 6$, $\sqrt{29}$ must be between 5 and 6.

Approximate each square root by finding the two whole numbers that it falls between.

$\sqrt{8}$ is between _____ and _____.

$\sqrt{35}$ is between _____ and _____.

$\sqrt{11}$ is between _____ and _____.

$\sqrt{70}$ is between _____ and _____.

$\sqrt{82}$ is between _____ and _____.

$\sqrt{26}$ is between _____ and _____.

$\sqrt{102}$ is between _____ and _____.

$\sqrt{99}$ is between _____ and _____.

$\sqrt{2}$ is between _____ and _____.

$\sqrt{135}$ is between _____ and _____.

$\sqrt{13}$ is between _____ and _____.

$\sqrt{24}$ is between _____ and _____.

$\sqrt{50}$ is between _____ and _____.

Learn!

You can find a better approximation for the square root of a non-perfect square by finding the two tenths that the square root falls between. You can plot your approximation on a number line.

Try it! Approximate $\sqrt{12}$ and plot your approximation on a number line.

First, find the two whole numbers the square root falls between.

$$9 < 12 < 16$$
$$\sqrt{9} < \sqrt{12} < \sqrt{16}$$
$$3 < \sqrt{12} < 4$$

Since $\sqrt{9} = 3$ and $\sqrt{16} = 4$, $\sqrt{12}$ must be between 3 and 4.

Now, choose decimals between 3 and 4, and square them to find the decimals that $\sqrt{12}$ falls between.

Since 12 is about halfway between 9 and 16, square a decimal about halfway between 3 and 4. Here, start with 3.5.

$3.5^2 = 12.25$ Since $3.5^2 > 12$, try a smaller decimal.
$3.4^2 = 11.56$

Since 12 is between 11.56 and 12.25, the square root of 12 must be between the square roots of those numbers.

$$\sqrt{11.56} < \sqrt{12} < \sqrt{12.25}$$

Since $\sqrt{11.56} = 3.4$ and $\sqrt{12.25} = 3.5$, $\sqrt{12}$ must be between 3.4 and 3.5.

Last, label a number line and plot your approximation.

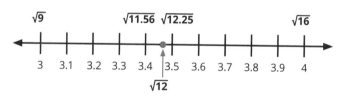

Approximate each square root by finding the two tenths it falls between. Then, label the number line and plot the approximation.

$\sqrt{21}$

$\sqrt{55}$

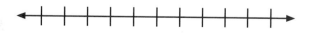

Learn!

If a whole number is not a perfect cube, its cube root is irrational. You can approximate the number's cube root by finding the two numbers that the cube root falls between.

Try it! Approximate $\sqrt[3]{100}$ by finding the two whole numbers that it falls between.

$64 < 100 < 125$ First, find the two nearest perfect cubes. The perfect cube just below 100 is 64. The perfect cube just above 100 is 125.

$\sqrt[3]{64} < \sqrt[3]{100} < \sqrt[3]{125}$ Then, find the cube root of the two nearest perfect cubes.

$4 < \sqrt[3]{100} < 5$ Since $\sqrt[3]{64} = 4$ and $\sqrt[3]{125} = 5$, $\sqrt[3]{100}$ must be between 4 and 5.

Approximate each cube root by finding the two whole numbers that it falls between.

$\sqrt[3]{3}$ is between _____ and _____.

$\sqrt[3]{40}$ is between _____ and _____.

$\sqrt[3]{362}$ is between _____ and _____.

$\sqrt[3]{28}$ is between _____ and _____.

$\sqrt[3]{914}$ is between _____ and _____.

$\sqrt[3]{785}$ is between _____ and _____.

$\sqrt[3]{16}$ is between _____ and _____.

$\sqrt[3]{600}$ is between _____ and _____.

$\sqrt[3]{6}$ is between _____ and _____.

$\sqrt[3]{315}$ is between _____ and _____.

$\sqrt[3]{832}$ is between _____ and _____.

$\sqrt[3]{180}$ is between _____ and _____.

DIG DEEPER! Think about how you would find a better approximation for $\sqrt[3]{40}$. What two tenths would it fall between?

Approximate each irrational number by finding the two tenths it falls between. Then label the number line and plot the approximation.

$5 + \sqrt{33}$

$\sqrt[3]{95}$

$\sqrt{103} - 2$

$3 + \sqrt{75}$

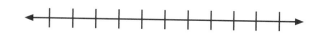

$\sqrt[3]{24}$

$\sqrt[3]{228}$

Get ahead of the curve with extra math practice! Join IXL today.

Scan the QR code for details.

Compare each pair of real numbers using > or <.

$\sqrt{18}$ ◯ $5.\overline{3}$ $4\frac{1}{3}$ ◯ $\sqrt{40}$

π ◯ $\dfrac{10}{2}$ 8.48 ◯ $\sqrt[3]{750}$

$-\dfrac{9}{4}$ ◯ $-\pi$ $\sqrt{50} - 5$ ◯ $1.\overline{81}$

$-\sqrt{2}$ ◯ -0.99 $\sqrt[3]{-11}$ ◯ $-\dfrac{11}{6}$

7.63 ◯ 2π $8\frac{1}{5} - \frac{4}{5}$ ◯ $\sqrt{65}$

$100 - \sqrt[3]{814}$ ◯ $90.\overline{1}$ $-\sqrt{30}$ ◯ $2 - 7.38$

Exploration Zone

You've worked with different types of real numbers, but did you know that there are **imaginary numbers** too? Imaginary numbers are not real and can be written using the value i. By definition, $i^2 = -1$. So, $i = \sqrt{-1}$. You can use i to think about the square root of negative numbers.

For example, $\sqrt{-25}$ is not real. It is imaginary. You can write the value of $\sqrt{-25}$ using i.

$\sqrt{-25} = \sqrt{(25)(-1)}$ First, write –25 as a product of two numbers, one of which is –1.

$= \sqrt{25} \cdot \sqrt{-1}$ Then, write the square root as a product of two square roots.

$= 5 \cdot \sqrt{-1}$ Next, evaluate $\sqrt{25}$.

$= 5i$ Last, rewrite $\sqrt{-1}$ as i.

So, $\sqrt{-25} = 5i$.

TRY IT YOURSELF!

Fill in the blanks to write $\sqrt{-9}$ using i.

$\sqrt{-9} = \sqrt{(\underline{})(-1)}$ First, write –9 as a product of two numbers, one of which is –1.

$= \sqrt{\underline{}} \cdot \sqrt{-1}$ Then, write the square root as a product of two square roots.

$= \underline{} \cdot \sqrt{-1}$ Next, evaluate the perfect square.

$= \underline{}$ Last, rewrite $\sqrt{-1}$ as i.

So, $\sqrt{-9} = \underline{}$.

Keep going! Fill in the blanks to write $\sqrt{-36}$ using i.

$\sqrt{-36} = \sqrt{(\underline{\hspace{0.5cm}})(-\underline{\hspace{0.5cm}})}$

$\phantom{\sqrt{-36}} = \sqrt{\underline{\hspace{0.5cm}}} \cdot \sqrt{-\underline{\hspace{0.5cm}}}$

$\phantom{\sqrt{-36}} = \underline{\hspace{0.5cm}} \cdot \sqrt{-\underline{\hspace{0.5cm}}}$

$\phantom{\sqrt{-36}} = \underline{\hspace{0.5cm}}$

So, $\sqrt{-36} = \underline{\hspace{0.5cm}}$.

Fill in the blanks to write $\sqrt{-64}$ using i.

$\sqrt{-64} = \sqrt{(\underline{\hspace{0.5cm}})(-\underline{\hspace{0.5cm}})}$

$\phantom{\sqrt{-64}} = \sqrt{\underline{\hspace{0.5cm}}} \cdot \sqrt{-\underline{\hspace{0.5cm}}}$

$\phantom{\sqrt{-64}} = \underline{\hspace{0.5cm}} \cdot \sqrt{-\underline{\hspace{0.5cm}}}$

$\phantom{\sqrt{-64}} = \underline{\hspace{0.5cm}}$

So, $\sqrt{-64} = \underline{\hspace{0.5cm}}$.

Learn!

Remember that an **exponent** tells you how many times the **base** is used as a factor. If the expression involves a negative, the parentheses will tell you how to evaluate it.

In $(-3)^4$, the base is -3.

$(-3)^4 = (-3) \cdot (-3) \cdot (-3) \cdot (-3) = 81$

In -3^4, the base is 3. The term is negative.

$-3^4 = -(3 \cdot 3 \cdot 3 \cdot 3) = -81$

Evaluate each expression.

$2^3 =$ _____

$(-6)^4 =$ _____

$-3^2 =$ _____

$-8^2 =$ _____

$(-20)^4 =$ _____

$-5^3 =$ _____

$4^4 =$ _____

$10^3 =$ _____

$(-7)^2 =$ _____

$(-50)^3 =$ _____

$\left(\dfrac{1}{3}\right)^2 =$ _____

$-9^4 =$ _____

$\left(-\dfrac{2}{7}\right)^2 =$ _____

$-3.5^2 =$ _____

IXL.com
skill ID
ZQC

Learn!

You can multiply with exponents using the following properties.

The **product of powers property** states that you can multiply powers with the same base by keeping the base and adding the exponents.

$$x^n \cdot x^m = x^{n+m}$$
$$4^2 \cdot 4^3 = 4^{2+3} = 4^5$$

To see why this property works, expand each power and simplify.

$$4^2 \cdot 4^3 = (4 \cdot 4)(4 \cdot 4 \cdot 4) = 4 \cdot 4 \cdot 4 \cdot 4 \cdot 4 = 4^5$$

The **power of a product property** states that you can find the power of a product by finding the power of each individual factor and multiplying.

$$(xy)^n = x^n \cdot y^n$$
$$(4 \cdot 3)^2 = 4^2 \cdot 3^2$$

To see why this property works, expand the power and simplify.

$$(4 \cdot 3)^2 = (4 \cdot 3)(4 \cdot 3) = (4 \cdot 4)(3 \cdot 3) = 4^2 \cdot 3^2$$

Simplify each expression. Express each product as a single power.

$5^6 \cdot 5^4 = \underline{\quad 5^{10} \quad}$

$8^4 \cdot 8^3 = \underline{\quad\quad}$

$9^7 \cdot 9^8 = \underline{\quad\quad}$

$(-4)^5 \cdot (-4)^2 = \underline{\quad\quad}$

$\left(\dfrac{2}{3}\right)^4 \cdot \left(\dfrac{2}{3}\right)^4 = \underline{\quad\quad}$

$10.25^6 \cdot 10.25^3 = \underline{\quad\quad}$

Expand each expression. Express each answer as the product of two powers.

$(6 \cdot 4)^5 = \underline{\quad 6^5 \cdot 4^5 \quad}$

$(10 \cdot 2)^7 = \underline{\quad\quad}$

$(3 \cdot 2.6)^8 = \underline{\quad\quad}$

$(6 \cdot (-7))^3 = \underline{\quad\quad}$

$\left(-\dfrac{3}{5} \cdot 2\dfrac{1}{4}\right)^2 = \underline{\quad\quad}$

IXL.com
skill ID
EQY

Learn!

The **power of a power property** states that you can find the power of a power by keeping the base and multiplying the exponents. This property can also be called the **power rule**.

$$(x^n)^m = x^{n \cdot m}$$

$$(4^2)^3 = 4^{2 \cdot 3} = 4^6$$

To see why this property works, expand each power and simplify.

$$(4^2)^3 = (4 \cdot 4)^3 = (4 \cdot 4)(4 \cdot 4)(4 \cdot 4) = 4 \cdot 4 \cdot 4 \cdot 4 \cdot 4 \cdot 4 = 4^6$$

Simplify each expression. Express each answer as a single power.

$(6^7)^3 = \underline{6^{21}}$

$(3^4)^5 = \underline{\hspace{2cm}}$

$(20^8)^2 = \underline{\hspace{2cm}}$

$(10^4)^4 = \underline{\hspace{2cm}}$

$(8^2)^5 = \underline{\hspace{2cm}}$

$(12^6)^3 = \underline{\hspace{2cm}}$

$(2^{10})^7 = \underline{\hspace{2cm}}$

$(4^6)^4 = \underline{\hspace{2cm}}$

$(9^{12})^5 = \underline{\hspace{2cm}}$

$(15^3)^8 = \underline{\hspace{2cm}}$

$(7^7)^8 = \underline{\hspace{2cm}}$

$(5^9)^{11} = \underline{\hspace{2cm}}$

$(0.9^4)^3 = \underline{\hspace{2cm}}$

$(18^{10})^{12} = \underline{\hspace{2cm}}$

$(11^5)^2 = \underline{\hspace{2cm}}$

$(13^6)^6 = \underline{\hspace{2cm}}$

$(0.23^6)^8 = \underline{\hspace{2cm}}$

$(4.18^4)^9 = \underline{\hspace{2cm}}$

$(25^7)^5 = \underline{\hspace{2cm}}$

$(0.09^4)^{11} = \underline{\hspace{2cm}}$

IXL.com
skill ID
AEQ

Learn!

The **quotient of powers property** states that you can divide powers with the same base by keeping the base and subtracting the exponents.

$$\frac{x^n}{x^m} = x^{n-m}$$

$$\frac{4^5}{4^3} = 4^{5-3} = 4^2$$

To see why this property works, expand each power and simplify.

$$\frac{4^5}{4^3} = \frac{4 \cdot 4 \cdot \cancel{4} \cdot \cancel{4} \cdot \cancel{4}}{\cancel{4} \cdot \cancel{4} \cdot \cancel{4}} = \frac{4 \cdot 4}{1} = 4^2$$

Simplify each expression. Express each answer as a single power.

$\dfrac{3^{10}}{3^2} = \underline{3^8}$

$\dfrac{9^5}{9^2} = \underline{\hspace{3cm}}$

$\dfrac{5^8}{5^3} = \underline{\hspace{3cm}}$

$\dfrac{12^{14}}{12^7} = \underline{\hspace{3cm}}$

$\dfrac{6^9}{6^3} = \underline{\hspace{3cm}}$

$\dfrac{2^{10}}{2^6} = \underline{\hspace{3cm}}$

$\dfrac{8^{12}}{8^4} = \underline{\hspace{3cm}}$

$\dfrac{10^6}{10^3} = \underline{\hspace{3cm}}$

$\dfrac{4^7}{4^2} = \underline{\hspace{3cm}}$

$\dfrac{15^{13}}{15^3} = \underline{\hspace{3cm}}$

$\dfrac{0.8^{20}}{0.8^8} = \underline{\hspace{3cm}}$

$\dfrac{30^9}{30^5} = \underline{\hspace{3cm}}$

$\dfrac{(-4)^{10}}{(-4)^3} = \underline{\hspace{3cm}}$

$\dfrac{80^{15}}{80^9} = \underline{\hspace{3cm}}$

$\dfrac{12.65^7}{12.65^4} = \underline{\hspace{3cm}}$

$\dfrac{7^{11}}{7^8} = \underline{\hspace{3cm}}$

$\dfrac{(-11)^{20}}{(-11)^{12}} = \underline{\hspace{3cm}}$

IXL.com
skill ID

M2C

Learn!

The **zero exponent property** states that any nonzero base raised to the power of zero is 1.

$$x^0 = 1$$
$$5^0 = 1$$

The **negative exponent property** states that you can write a power with a negative exponent as a fraction with 1 in the numerator and a positive exponent in the denominator.

$$x^{-n} = \frac{1}{x^n}$$

$$5^{-2} = \frac{1}{5^2}$$

Use the properties above to simplify each expression.

$2^{-5} = \underline{\quad \frac{1}{2^5} \quad}$

$9^{-3} = \underline{\qquad}$

$(-12)^0 = \underline{\qquad}$

$3^{-8} = \underline{\qquad}$

$35^0 = \underline{\qquad}$

$5.6^0 = \underline{\qquad}$

$20^{-6} = \underline{\qquad}$

$(-8)^0 = \underline{\qquad}$

$11^{-4} = \underline{\qquad}$

$\left(\frac{7}{9}\right)^0 = \underline{\qquad}$

$60^0 = \underline{\qquad}$

$19^{-2} = \underline{\qquad}$

$83^{-7} = \underline{\qquad}$

$(-10)^{-10} = \underline{\qquad}$

$-7^0 = \underline{\qquad}$

IXL.com
skill ID
5MA

$\left(\frac{3}{11}\right)^0 = \underline{\qquad}$

$999^{-3} = \underline{\qquad}$

How can you prove that the zero exponent property and the negative exponent property work? Follow the directions below.

Show why the zero exponent property works by filling in the missing number in each box.

Any nonzero number divided by itself is equal to 1.

Subtract to solve.

$$1 = \frac{n^3}{n^3} = n^{\boxed{} - \boxed{}} = n^{\boxed{}}$$

Use the quotient of powers property.

You can see that all of the expressions are equal to one another. Write an equation to show that the expression you started with is equal to the expression you ended with.

_____ = _____

Your equation shows the zero exponent property. So, you've proved that the property works!

Show why the negative exponent property works by filling in the missing number in each box.

The zero exponent property shows that $n^0 = 1$.

Subtract to solve.

$$\frac{1}{n^4} = \frac{n^0}{n^4} = n^{\boxed{} - \boxed{}} = n^{\boxed{}}$$

Use the quotient of powers property.

Again, you can see that all of the expressions are equal to one another. Write an equation to show that the expression you started with is equal to the expression you ended with.

_____ = _____

Your equation shows the negative exponent property. So, you've proved that the property works!

Use the properties of exponents to simplify each expression. Express each answer as a single term with a positive exponent.

$3^5 \cdot 3^8 =$ _____

$(8^6)^2 =$ _____

$\dfrac{0.03^8}{0.03^3} =$ _____

$9^{-2} =$ _____

$(4.2^7)^3 =$ _____

$\dfrac{(-14)^{20}}{(-14)^{10}} =$ _____

$4.5^4 \cdot 4.5^2 =$ _____

$(11^5)^4 =$ _____

$(5.127^3)^4 =$ _____

$\dfrac{3^{17}}{3^{15}} =$ _____

$(-2)^{-8} =$ _____

$(-12)^6 \cdot (-12)^3 =$ _____

$\dfrac{9^{15}}{9^8} =$ _____

$\left(\dfrac{1}{7}\right)^2 \cdot \left(\dfrac{1}{7}\right)^5 =$ _____

$(-35)^{-6} =$ _____

$(9.17^4)^4 =$ _____

$(-12)^{-7} =$ _____

$\dfrac{(-6.87)^{14}}{(-6.87)^5} =$ _____

Draw a line between each pair of equivalent expressions.

8^0 $(-10)^{10}$

$8^4 \cdot 8^5$ 17^8

17^{-6} 8^{10}

$(-10)^5 \cdot (-10)^5$ $\dfrac{1}{(-10)^4}$

$(8^5)^4$ $(-10)^9$

$17^3 \cdot 17^5$ 8^9

$(-10)^{-4}$ 17^{15}

$\dfrac{17^{11}}{17^5}$ 17^6

$\dfrac{(-10)^{17}}{(-10)^8}$ 1

$(17^5)^3$ 8^{20}

$\dfrac{8^{12}}{8^2}$ $\dfrac{1}{17^6}$

Simplify each expression using the properties of exponents. Write each answer as a single term with a positive exponent.

$(5^4)^2 \cdot 5^8 =$ _____

$\dfrac{8^2}{8^7} =$ _____

$\dfrac{(-7)^8}{(-7)^3 \cdot (-7)^2} =$ _____

$\dfrac{(-20)^{20}}{(-20)^{12}} \cdot (-20)^3 =$ _____

$\dfrac{11^1}{11^{16}} =$ _____

$\dfrac{8.12^{12}}{8.12^7} \cdot \dfrac{8.12^{10}}{8.12^3} =$ _____

$\dfrac{0.38^3 \cdot 0.38^9}{0.38^8} =$ _____

$(45^5)^2 \cdot (45^2)^3 =$ _____

$(2.5^4)^2 \cdot (2.5^3)^4 =$ _____

$\dfrac{(-9)^5}{(-9)^{10} \cdot (-9)^4} =$ _____

Challenge!

IXL.com
Checkpoint ID

GEJ

Learn!

You can approximate a very large or very small number by rounding the number and writing it as the product of a single digit and a power of 10. You can use ≈ to mean approximately equal to.

Try it! The distance between the Earth and the moon is about 238,900 miles.

$238{,}900 \approx 200{,}000$ To approximate this number, first round to the nearest 100,000.

$200{,}000 = 2 \times 100{,}000$ Now, write the rounded number as a product of a single digit and a power of 10. Count the zeros in 100,000 to determine the exponent on its power of 10.

$= 2 \times 10^5$ So, the distance between the Earth and the moon is about 2×10^5 miles.

Now try it with another number! Bamboo grows at a rate of about 0.000031 miles per hour.

$0.000031 \approx 0.00003$ To approximate this number, first round to the nearest 0.00001.

$0.00003 = 3 \times 0.00001$ Now, write the rounded number as a product of a single digit and a power of 10. Count the digits after the decimal point in 0.00001 to determine the exponent on its power of 10.

$= 3 \times 10^{-5}$ So, bamboo grows at a rate of about 3×10^{-5} miles per hour.

Approximate the numbers using a power of 10.

The circumference of Jupiter is about 439,000 kilometers.

The mass of a grain of sand is about 0.000016 grams.

Light travels through water at a speed of about 226,000,000 meters per second.

The diameter of a water molecule is about 0.000000028 centimeters.

Learn!

You can write very large and very small numbers using **scientific notation**. In scientific notation, the first factor must be greater than or equal to 1 and less than 10. The second factor must be a power of 10. Here are examples of numbers in scientific notation and standard form:

$$9.2 \times 10^7 = 92{,}000{,}000 \qquad 4.03 \times 10^{-6} = 0.00000403$$

To convert a number from scientific notation to standard form, look at the exponent in the power of 10 to see how many places to move the decimal point in the first factor. If the exponent is positive, move the decimal point to the right. If the exponent is negative, move the decimal point to the left.

Try it! Write each number in standard form.

3.82×10^6	Move the decimal point 6 places to the right, adding in zeros as needed.
3.820000	
	So, $3.82 \times 10^6 = 3{,}820{,}000$.

7×10^{-5}	Move the decimal point 5 places to the left, adding in zeros as needed.
00007.	
	So, $7 \times 10^{-5} = 0.00007$.

Write each number in standard form.

$4.3 \times 10^5 =$ _____

$9.1 \times 10^{-3} =$ _____

$7 \times 10^7 =$ _____

$2 \times 10^{-4} =$ _____

$5.5 \times 10^{-9} =$ _____

$6.7 \times 10^8 =$ _____

$3 \times 10^{-8} =$ _____

$9.6 \times 10^5 =$ _____

$4.45 \times 10^6 =$ _____

$7.03 \times 10^{-7} =$ _____

Learn!

You can also convert a number from standard form to scientific notation.

To find the first factor, move the decimal point left or right until you form a number that is greater than or equal to 1 and less than 10.

To find the exponent in the power of 10, count the number of places you moved the decimal point and follow these rules:

- If you moved the decimal point to the left, the exponent will be positive.
- If you moved the decimal point to the right, the exponent will be negative.

Let's try it! Write each number in scientific notation.

600,000,000

600,000,000.

Move the decimal point after the 6. The first factor will be 6.

You moved the decimal point 8 places to the left, so the exponent will be 8.

So, $600,000,000 = 6 \times 10^8$.

0.00012

0.00012

Move the decimal point after the 1. The first factor will be 1.2.

You moved the decimal point 4 places to the right, so the exponent will be -4.

So, $0.00012 = 1.2 \times 10^{-4}$.

Write each number in scientific notation.

9,000,000 = _____

0.00000083 = _____

65,000,000 = _____

0.004 = _____

0.00000008 = _____

220,000,000 = _____

1,000,000,000 = _____

0.000002031 = _____

0.000000000041 = _____

50,700,000,000 = _____

Convert between scientific notation and standard form to fill in the blanks.

5×10^{-9} = _____

_____ = 0.00003

1.3×10^{8} = _____

7×10^{10} = _____

_____ = 70,000,000

_____ = 0.000000055

_____ = 800,000

8.7×10^{-6} = _____

3×10^{7} = _____

_____ = 360,000,000

4.36×10^{6} = _____

_____ = 0.0000000061

_____ = 1,750,000,000

7.6×10^{-7} = _____

2.2×10^{-8} = _____

_____ = 1,500,000

IXL.com
skill ID

H8A

For more practice, visit IXL.com or the IXL mobile app and enter this code in the search bar.

Compare each pair of numbers using >, <, or =.

0.00006 ◯ 6×10^{-4} 8.4×10^{7} ◯ $8{,}400{,}000$

0.00000075 ◯ 7.5×10^{-8} 9.92×10^{-6} ◯ 0.00000992

5×10^{9} ◯ $500{,}000{,}000$ $63{,}000{,}000$ ◯ 6.3×10^{6}

0.000000013 ◯ 1.3×10^{-10} 4.48×10^{4} ◯ $44{,}800$

0.00000000877 ◯ 8.77×10^{-9} 3.9×10^{8} ◯ $39{,}000{,}000{,}000$

2.5×10^{-3} ◯ 0.00025 0.0000072 ◯ 7.2×10^{-7}

$115{,}000{,}000{,}000$ ◯ 1.15×10^{12} 3.65×10^{-6} ◯ 0.0000365

4×10^{8} ◯ 6×10^{7} 5.89×10^{10} ◯ $589{,}000{,}000{,}000$

Answer each question.

Scientists estimate that Earth has approximately
3,500,000,000,000 fish in the ocean. Scientists also
estimate that there are approximately 2×10^{16} ants on
Earth. Which is the larger estimate?

fish in the ocean

ants on Earth

A grain of sugar weighs about 6.25×10^{-4} grams. A grain
of salt weighs about 0.000058 grams. Which is heavier?

grain of sugar

grain of salt

A scientist is looking at a plant cell under a microscope.
The cell's nucleus is about 5.1×10^{-4} centimeters long.
One of the cell's mitochondria is about 1.9×10^{-4}
centimeters long. One of the cell's chloroplasts is about
0.0005 centimeters long. List those three parts of the cell
in order from shortest to longest.

_____

_____

_____

A paleontologist is examining four dinosaur fossils.
Fossil A is estimated to be 6.5×10^{7} years old. Fossil B is
estimated to be 5.9×10^{8} years old. Fossil C is estimated
to be 680,000,000 years old. Fossil D is estimated to be
60,000,000 years old. List the four fossils in order from
oldest to youngest.

_____

_____

_____

_____

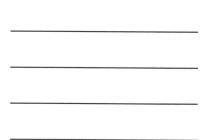

Learn!

You can add and subtract numbers in scientific notation using the distributive property.

Try it! Add $(8.3 \times 10^7) + (6.2 \times 10^7)$.

$= (8.3 + 6.2) \times 10^7$ Apply the distributive property.

$= 14.5 \times 10^7$ Simplify.

$= (1.45 \times 10) \times 10^7$ Rewrite your answer in scientific notation, if needed.

$= 1.45 \times 10^8$

Add or subtract. Write your answer in scientific notation.

$(9.5 \times 10^3) - (6.4 \times 10^3) = \underline{\quad 3.1 \times 10^3 \quad}$ $(6.4 \times 10^8) + (2.3 \times 10^8) = \underline{\qquad\qquad}$

$(9.5 - 6.4) \times 10^3$

3.1×10^3

$(5.1 \times 10^{-7}) - (2.8 \times 10^{-7}) = \underline{\qquad\qquad}$ $(5 \times 10^{10}) + (1.8 \times 10^{10}) = \underline{\qquad\qquad}$

$(1.99 \times 10^{-5}) + (8.4 \times 10^{-5}) = \underline{\qquad\qquad}$ $(8 \times 10^{-9}) - (3.7 \times 10^{-9}) = \underline{\qquad\qquad}$

$(8.7 \times 10^6) + (7.6 \times 10^6) = \underline{\qquad\qquad}$ $(5.13 \times 10^{-6}) - (4.8 \times 10^{-6}) = \underline{\qquad\qquad}$

$(7.85 \times 10^{-10}) + (7.106 \times 10^{-10}) = \underline{\qquad\qquad}$ $(9.5 \times 10^9) - (8.975 \times 10^9) = \underline{\qquad\qquad}$

Learn!

To add or subtract numbers in scientific notation that have different powers of 10, rewrite the numbers to have the same power of 10 before adding or subtracting.

Try it! Subtract $(9.53 \times 10^6) - (2.2 \times 10^5)$.

$= [(9.53 \times 10) \times 10^5] - (2.2 \times 10^5)$ Since the numbers do not have the same power of 10, rewrite one of the numbers so that they do. It's easier to rewrite the number with the greater power of 10.

$= (95.3 \times 10^5) - (2.2 \times 10^5)$

$= (95.3 - 2.2) \times 10^5$ Apply the distributive property.

$= 93.1 \times 10^5$ Simplify.

$= (9.31 \times 10) \times 10^5$ Rewrite your answer in scientific notation, if needed.

$= 9.31 \times 10^6$

Add or subtract. Write your answer in scientific notation.

$(7 \times 10^5) + (1.5 \times 10^6) =$ _____

$(7.25 \times 10^5) - (9.6 \times 10^4) =$ _____

$(4 \times 10^{-6}) - (1.1 \times 10^{-7}) =$ _____

$(6.5 \times 10^{-9}) + (1.7 \times 10^{-10}) =$ _____

$(4.98 \times 10^{10}) + (4.67 \times 10^8) =$ _____

$(3.95 \times 10^6) + (7.2 \times 10^4) =$ _____

IXL.com
skill ID
HUR

$(9.2 \times 10^{-8}) - (3.57 \times 10^{-9}) =$ _____

Add or subtract. Write your answer in scientific notation.

$(7.7 \times 10^5) - (6.9 \times 10^5) =$ _____ $(8.31 \times 10^{10}) + (4.5 \times 10^9) =$ _____

$(5.6 \times 10^{-7}) - (9.33 \times 10^{-8}) =$ _____ $(3.48 \times 10^8) + (6.72 \times 10^8) =$ _____

$(2.89 \times 10^5) + (8.16 \times 10^6) =$ _____ $(7.046 \times 10^{-5}) + (7.28 \times 10^{-5}) =$ _____

$(3.25 \times 10^{-7}) - (1.9 \times 10^{-7}) =$ _____ $(4.86 \times 10^{10}) - (5.6 \times 10^8) =$ _____

$(8.8 \times 10^{10}) + (9.5 \times 10^{10}) =$ _____ $(1.38 \times 10^{-4}) - (6.25 \times 10^{-6}) =$ _____

$(4.06 \times 10^{-7}) - (3.97 \times 10^{-7}) =$ _____ $(5.315 \times 10^{-9}) + (1.28 \times 10^{-8}) =$ _____

Learn!

You can multiply numbers in scientific notation.

Try it! Multiply $(5.2 \times 10^8)(7 \times 10^3)$.

$= (5.2 \times 7)(10^8 \times 10^3)$	Group the first factors together and the powers of 10 together.
$= 36.4 \times (10^8 \times 10^3)$	Multiply the first factors.
$= 36.4 \times 10^{11}$	Multiply the powers of 10 by adding the exponents.
$= 3.64 \times 10^{12}$	Rewrite your answer in scientific notation, if needed.

Multiply. Write your answer in scientific notation.

$(2.4 \times 10^5)(1.8 \times 10^6) =$ _____

$(3 \times 10^4)(2.3 \times 10^{10}) =$ _____

$(4.5 \times 10^8)(7 \times 10^3) =$ _____

$(5.2 \times 10^9)(1.7 \times 10^9) =$ _____

$(6 \times 10^7)(5.36 \times 10^{-10}) =$ _____

$(1.2 \times 10^{-6})(9.8 \times 10^{-4}) =$ _____

$(7.55 \times 10^{-8})(3 \times 10^6) =$ _____

Learn!

You can also divide numbers in scientific notation.

Try it! Divide $\dfrac{5.1 \times 10^{10}}{6 \times 10^{7}}$.

$= \dfrac{5.1}{6} \times \dfrac{10^{10}}{10^{7}}$ Group the first factors together and the powers of 10 together.

$= 0.85 \times \dfrac{10^{10}}{10^{7}}$ Divide the first factors.

$= 0.85 \times 10^{3}$ Divide the powers of 10 by subtracting the exponents.

$= 8.5 \times 10^{2}$ Rewrite your answer in scientific notation, if needed.

Divide. Write your answer in scientific notation.

$\dfrac{5.6 \times 10^{8}}{5 \times 10^{4}} = $ _____

$\dfrac{9.42 \times 10^{10}}{3 \times 10^{4}} = $ _____

$\dfrac{7.8 \times 10^{7}}{4 \times 10^{2}} = $ _____

$\dfrac{2.45 \times 10^{9}}{7 \times 10^{3}} = $ _____

$\dfrac{8.55 \times 10^{-10}}{6 \times 10^{-7}} = $ _____

$\dfrac{5.1 \times 10^{6}}{1.2 \times 10^{-2}} = $ _____

$\dfrac{1.425 \times 10^{-5}}{1.5 \times 10^{8}} = $ _____

IXL.com
skill ID
SGT

Add, subtract, multiply, or divide. Write your answer in scientific notation.

$(4.92 \times 10^4) + (3.7 \times 10^5) =$ _____

$\dfrac{3.15 \times 10^8}{5 \times 10^3} =$ _____

$(3.8 \times 10^5)(6.1 \times 10^7) =$ _____

$(8.15 \times 10^{-6}) - (4.9 \times 10^{-6}) =$ _____

$(8.4 \times 10^{-10})(9.2 \times 10^3) =$ _____

$(5.05 \times 10^{-9}) + (9.31 \times 10^{-9}) =$ _____

$(2.35 \times 10^8) - (1.848 \times 10^7) =$ _____

$\dfrac{8.12 \times 10^{-5}}{1.4 \times 10^3} =$ _____

$(4 \times 10^{-8})(3.99 \times 10^4) =$ _____

$(9 \times 10^7) + (6.27 \times 10^5) =$ _____

Answer each question. Write your answer in scientific notation.

Scientists estimate that there are approximately 4×10^5 distinct flower species. Scientists also estimate that there are approximately 1.75×10^4 distinct butterfly species. How many more distinct flower species are there estimated to be than distinct butterfly species?

_____

A piece of paper is 3.9×10^{-3} inches thick. What would be the total thickness, in inches, of a stack of 5×10^5 pieces of paper?

_____

An asteroid is headed toward the sun. It is currently 2.97×10^8 miles from the sun, and it is traveling at a speed of 4×10^4 miles per hour. If the asteroid keeps traveling in the same direction at the same speed, how many hours will it take the asteroid to reach the sun?

_____

Mr. Gabriel combines 1.4×10^{-4} kilograms of copper and 9.7×10^{-5} kilograms of zinc to create a brass alloy for a craft project. What is the mass, in kilograms, of the brass alloy?

_____

Solve each equation for the variable. Remember that you can use inverse operations to solve equations.

$2h + 3 = 9$

$-6 + 3d = 12$

$-2 = 8p + 14$

$5 - 4c = 13$

$3 = -2y + 7$

$6b + 20 = 2$

$8r - 6 = 18$

$14 - 3s = -19$

$4 = 5n - 18$

$8.2 = -2m + 3.4$

$\dfrac{z}{3} + 5 = 3$

$\dfrac{u + 8}{2} = 12$

$2 = 3j - 8$

$\dfrac{2}{3}a + 23 = 31$

Learn!

When you have an equation with like terms on the same side, you can combine the like terms before solving.

Try it! Solve $2n + 5 - 4n = 17$.

$$2n + 5 - 4n = 17$$

First, find the like terms on the same side of the equation. Here, $2n$ and $-4n$ are like terms. Then, combine the like terms.

$$-2n + 5 = 17$$

$$-2n + 5 - 5 = 17 - 5$$

Use inverse operations to solve for n.

$$\frac{-2n}{-2} = \frac{12}{-2}$$

$$n = -6$$

Solve each equation for the variable.

$3b + 2b = 10$

$6q + 5q = 33$

$2s - 15s = 26$

$6x + 2x - 9x = 15$

$-4y + 3y - 8 = -19$

$2u + 5u = 12$

$1.5t - 3.5t = -8.4$

$\frac{1}{2}p + \frac{3}{8}p - \frac{3}{4}p = 5$

IXL.com
skill ID
Q2B

Learn!

When you have an equation with the same variable on both sides, you can use inverse operations to move all like variable terms to one side of the equation.

Try it! Solve $5h + 1 = -3h + 17$.

$5h + 1 = -3h + 17$ The variable terms $5h$ and $-3h$ are on opposite sides.

$5h + 3h + 1 = -3h + 3h + 17$ Add $3h$ to both sides to get the variable terms together. Then, simplify by combining like terms.

$8h + 1 = 17$ Use inverse operations to solve for h.

$8h = 16$

$h = 2$

Solve each equation for the variable.

$1 + 5w = w + 13$ $9s + 3 = 8s + 4$ $-2y + 8 = -5y - 7$

$11c - 9 = 15 + 9c$ $4b + 18 = b + 36$

IXL.com
skill ID
ZYL

Keep going! Solve each equation for the variable. Be sure to first combine any like terms.

$-12 + 12z = 16 + 8z$

$18k - 18 = 3k + 27$

$2b - 14 = -15 + 5b - 8$

$3m + 5m - 3 = 2m + 27$

$18q - 4q + 19 = 10q + 31$

$\frac{1}{6}s + 13 = 19 + \frac{1}{3}s$

$28 + 10d = 4d + 20$

$0.2t + 1.7 = 3.5 - 0.2t$

$-15 - 14j = -12j + 12$

$c - \frac{3}{4} = \frac{1}{2}c + \frac{1}{4}c + 1$

$1.3p - 7.5p - 4.6 = 9 - 6.4p$

IXL.com
skill ID
UEM

Learn!

When you have an equation with parentheses, you can use the distributive property to help you solve the equation.

Try it! Solve $2(s - 6) + 4 = 16$.

$2(s - 6) + 4 = 16$	Use the distributive property to rewrite the equation. Distribute 2 to each of the terms inside the parentheses. Then, simplify.
$2(s) + 2(-6) + 4 = 16$	
$2s - 12 + 4 = 16$	Combine like terms on the same side of the equation.
$2s - 8 = 16$	Use inverse operations to solve for s.
$2s = 24$	
$s = 12$	

Solve each equation for the variable.

$3(g - 8) = -12$ $-5(2f + 7) = 45$ $11(k + 5) - 15 = 7$

$-6(3x - 2) + 10 = 22$ $4(b - 7) + 8b = -20$ $7(3u + 6.3) - 2.8 = 9.8$

SOLVE IT A DIFFERENT WAY! Try solving the equation $3(g - 8) = -12$ by dividing both sides of the equation by 3 first. You should get the same answer as you did above!

Keep going! Solve each equation for the variable.

$-2(g + 7) - 13g = -89$

$6(y - 2) + y = -40$

$9 = 19(x - 1) - 10$

$-4(5m + 4) - 15 = 29$

$-2 = 3(t - 4) + 5t$

$7(3n + 3) + 13 = -8$

$220 = -20(6f + 4) - 100$

$0.9(2w + 3.1) + 4.4 = 11.15$

$4\left(-5j + \dfrac{1}{2}\right) - 8 = -36$

$3.5(c - 8) + 2 = -21.1$

$5 = 8\left(\dfrac{1}{2}a + \dfrac{1}{6}\right) - \dfrac{2}{3}$

IXL.com
skill ID
8RP

Time for review! Solve each equation for the variable.

$2w + 8 = 3w + 2w - 10$ $y + 2y - 7 = 4y + 5$ $4(d + 2) - 3d = 14$

$-2(g - 5) = 3g - 15$ $5t + 3(t + 2) = 22$ $3(p - 1) + 2(p + 3) = -7$

$4(2v - 4) = 2v + 26$ $2(3b + 5) + 5b = 6(2b - 1)$ $5(a - 4) - 3a = 2(4a + 2)$

$3 = 2(5n - 2) - 3(4n + 1)$ $8q - 4 = 4q + 2(3q - 2)$

IXL.com
skill ID
55K

Keep going! Solve each equation for the variable.

$4a + 7 = 6a - 3a + 19$

$2v - 1.5 = -v + 5v + 8.5$

$3(2n + 6) - 2(2n - 4) = 4$

$7x - 2(2x + 7) + 4x = 42$

$15s + 4(s + 5) = 44 + 27s$

$3z + 7 = 8z - 11 - 4z$

$2(4m - 3) = 8m - 6m$

$-(b + 1.2) + 3b = 2.6$

$\dfrac{3}{4}p + 2(p - 1) = 3p$

$1.5(3w + 5) + 4.5w = 7(2w - 1)$

$\dfrac{7}{4}(t - 2) - 3t = -\dfrac{9}{2}$

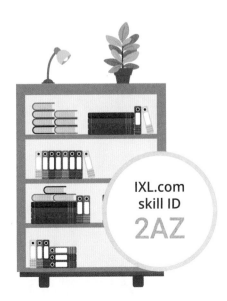

IXL.com
skill ID
2AZ

Find a path from start to finish. Step only on spaces that have solutions greater than 1. No diagonal moves are allowed.

START

$3(3j - 4) + 2 = 8j + 9$	$2(3t + 5) = 4t - 8$	$\frac{2}{3}(w - 3) + 2w = 5$
$1.2(h + 4) = 3(h - 2.6)$	$-1.3a + 2.4(a + 4) = 11.8$	$x + 4 - 2x = 4x + 3$
$4(n + 2) = 3n - 2n + 5$	$-4c + 2c + 8 = 3c + 2$	$\frac{4}{5}f + \frac{1}{2}\left(f + \frac{1}{3}\right) = \frac{1}{6}$
$-8(z + 5) - (z + 2) = -15$	$3r + 2(r - 3) - 4r = -4$	$-5 + 2(p - 6) = -3p$

FINISH

Write an equation for each problem. Then, solve.

Alana is shopping for a pair of jeans and some T-shirts. She bought a pair of jeans for $40 and some T-shirts for $8.50 each. She spent $74 altogether before tax. How many T-shirts did Alana buy?

$$8.5x + 40 = 74$$
$$8.5x = 34$$
$$x = 4$$

$\underline{\text{4 T-shirts}}$

Julia is having her birthday party at the aquarium. Each aquarium ticket costs $11.50, and lunch costs $8 per person. Julia's mom also buys a cake for $38.50. Altogether, Julia's birthday party costs $214. How many people are at Julia's party?

_____

Violet and Owen are both hiking on Scout's Peak Trail. When Violet starts on the trail, Owen has already hiked 1.5 miles. Violet is hiking at a pace of 3.8 miles per hour, and Owen is hiking at a pace of 2.6 miles per hour. If they both keep hiking the trail at these rates, how long will it take Violet to catch up to Owen?

_____

Anthony and Riley both went to the movies with their families last night. Anthony's family bought 4 movie tickets and spent $32 on snacks. Riley's family bought 3 movie tickets and spent $13 on snacks. Anthony's family spent $30 more than Riley's family. If all tickets cost the same amount, what is the price of one movie ticket?

_____

Learn!

Linear equations can have one solution, no solution, or infinitely many solutions. Look at the examples below.

If an equation is true for a single value of the variable, then it has exactly **one solution**.

The equation $3x + 1 = 4x - 2$ has exactly one solution. When you solve the equation, you get one value for x.

$$3x + 1 = 4x - 2$$
$$3x + 1 + 2 = 4x - 2 + 2$$
$$3x + 3 = 4x$$
$$3x - 3x + 3 = 4x - 3x$$
$$3 = x$$

If an equation is false for all values of the variable, then it has **no solution**.

The equation $3x + 1 = 3x - 2$ has no solution. When you solve the equation, you get a false statement. No matter what value is substituted for x, the equation is false.

$$3x + 1 = 3x - 2$$
$$3x - 3x + 1 = 3x - 3x - 2$$
$$1 = -2$$

If an equation is true for all values of the variable, then it has **infinitely many solutions**.

The equation $3x + 1 = 3x + 1$ has infinitely many solutions. When you solve the equation, you get a true statement. No matter what value is substituted for x, the equation is true.

$$3x + 1 = 3x + 1$$
$$3x - 3x + 1 = 3x - 3x + 1$$
$$1 = 1$$

Determine whether each equation has one solution, no solution, or infinitely many solutions.

$$2b + 9 = 5b - 6$$

$$-3 + 6j = 6j - 3$$

one solution

$$-s + 10 = 4 - s$$

IXL.com
skill ID

XDE

Keep going! Determine whether each equation has one solution, no solution, or infinitely many solutions.

$2(2f + 5) = 3f + 7$

$6h + 15 = 9h - 3$

_____

_____

$5(2 - 2c) = -10c + 10$

$7g - 2 - g = 6g + 10$

_____

_____

$7d - 2 + 2d = 9d - 2$

$3(3j - 7) = 3 + 3j$

_____

_____

$4(q - 1) + 4 = 4q - 4$

$3(2 - 4w) + 4w - 5 = 1 - 8w$

_____

_____

$-2(5y - 3) = 6 - 10y$

$2(8k - 7) - k - 3 = 3(5k - 6)$

_____

_____

Find the path from start to finish.

If the equation has one solution, move one square down.

If the equation has no solution, move one square to the left.

If the equation has infinitely many solutions, move one square to the right.

START ↓

$2(3x - 5) + x = 7x - 10$	$4(3 - x) = -5x + 9$	$6x - 8 + 2x = 8x - 8$
$-5(-x + 2) + 3x + 2 = 4(2x - 8)$	$-3(2x + 4) + 4x + 2 = 3x + 5$	$4(10 - x) - 8 = -4x + 8$
$2(8 - x) + 2 = x + 3$	$3(3x - 1) - 5x - 3 = 2(2x + 9)$	$-(9x + 9) = 10 - 9x$
$-(x + 6) + 6x + 1 = 5x - 5$	$7x - 3 - 3x = 4x - 3$	$3(4x - 5) - 7 = 4 - x$
$-6(1 - 2x) + 2x - 1 = 7(2x - 1)$	$5(3x + 2) - 7x = 8x + 2$	$-2(2x + 9) - 6x = 9x + 1$

↓ FINISH

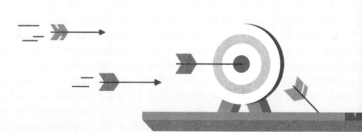

Fill in each blank with a number that creates an equation with infinitely many solutions.

$10x + 4 = 10x +$ _____

_____ $x - 9 = 3x - 9$

$-5x + 6 =$ _____ $x + 6$

$-4x + 10 =$ _____ $- 4x$

_____ $x = 3x + 4x$

$8x - 6 -$ _____ $x = 6x - 6$

Fill in each blank with a number that creates an equation with no solution.

_____ $x = 4x + 9$

$8x - 4 =$ _____ $x + 2$

$6x + 1 - 2x =$ _____ $x + 3$

$2(-3x + 5) = 1 -$ _____ x

$-x + 6 + 3x = 2x +$ _____

$-x +$ _____ $= 3x - 4x$

DIG DEEPER! The last two problems on this page have more than one correct answer. For each of those problems, find a number that is **not** a correct answer.

IXL.com skill ID

7TY

Learn!

In a proportional relationship, the ratio of *y* to *x* is the constant of proportionality, *k*.

If you have a proportional relationship, you can calculate the constant of proportionality using the equation $k = \frac{y}{x}$. Then you can write an equation in the form $y = kx$ to represent the proportional relationship.

Find each constant of proportionality. Then write an equation to represent each proportional relationship.

x	1	2	3
y	4	8	12

Equation: ___$y = 4x$___

x	3	6	9
y	1	2	3

Equation: _____

x	2	3	5
y	4	6	10

Equation: _____

x	2	4	6
y	3	6	9

Equation: _____

x	10	15	25
y	2	3	5

Equation: _____

x	10	20	40
y	6	12	24

Equation: _____

x	3	9	12
y	4	12	16

Equation: _____

Find each constant of proportionality. Then write an equation to represent each proportional relationship.

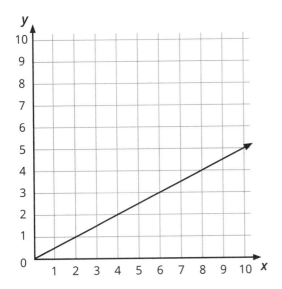

Equation: $y = \dfrac{1}{2}x$

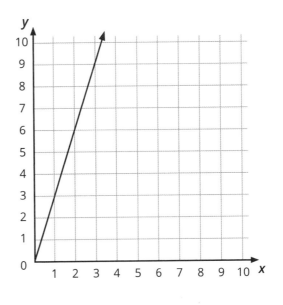

Equation: _____

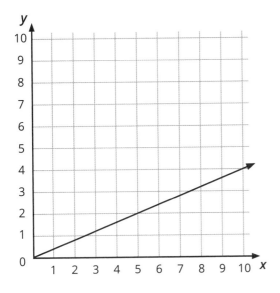

Equation: _____

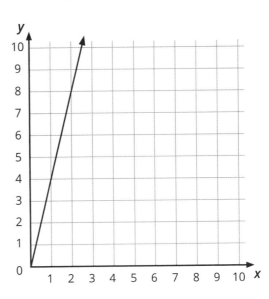

Equation: _____

Compare the proportional relationships in each problem. Use each constant of proportionality to help you.

Greener Pastures Farm sells cheese by weight. The table shows the cost for Brie cheese, and the graph shows the cost for cheddar cheese.

Weight of Brie (oz.)	Cost
6	$15
8	$20
10	$25

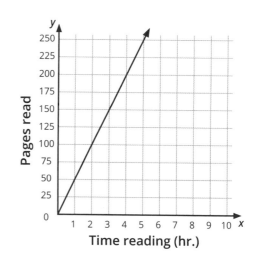

Weight of cheddar (oz.)

What is the cost per ounce of Brie? _____

What is the cost per ounce of cheddar? _____

Which cheese is less expensive? _____

Kiara and Mya's book club read a science fiction book last month.

The graph to the right shows the rate at which Mya read the book.

The equation $y = 45x$ models the rate at which Kiara read the book, where x is the time spent reading, in hours, and y is the pages read.

Time reading (hr.)

How many pages per hour did Kiara read? _____

How many pages per hour did Mya read? _____

Who read faster? _____

Keep going! Compare the proportional relationships in each problem.

Paddle Paradise rents kayaks and paddleboards by the hour.

The equation $y = 12x$ models the cost for renting a kayak, where x is the number of hours and y is the cost in dollars.

Paddle Paradise charges $91 to rent a paddleboard for 7 hours.

What is the cost per hour of renting a kayak? _____

What is the cost per hour of renting a paddleboard? _____

Which rental is more expensive? _____

Tomas is decorating cookies shaped like diplomas and graduation caps for a graduation party.

The table shows the rate at which Tomas decorates diploma cookies.

The equation $y = 1.5x$ models the rate at which Tomas decorates graduation cap cookies, where x is the number of cookies decorated and y is the number of minutes spent decorating.

Number of diploma cookies	12	24	36
Time spent decorating (min.)	30	60	90

How many minutes does it take Tomas to decorate each graduation cap cookie?

_____

How many minutes does it take Tomas to decorate each diploma cookie?

_____

Which type of cookie can Tomas decorate faster? _____

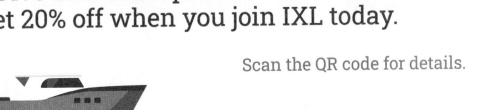

Learn!

The slope of a line measures the line's steepness. You can find the slope of a line by determining the ratio of the **change in y**, called the **rise**, over the **change in x**, called the **run**. Slope is generally expressed as a simplified fraction or integer.

$$\text{Slope} = \frac{\text{change in } y}{\text{change in } x} = \frac{\text{rise}}{\text{run}}$$

Try it! Find the slope of the proportional relationship on the graph.

First, choose any two points on the line. Determine the rise and run between the two points. Here, the rise is **1**. The run is **2**.

Now, write the ratio of rise to run.

$$\text{Slope} = \frac{1}{2}$$

So, the slope of the proportional relationship is $\frac{1}{2}$.

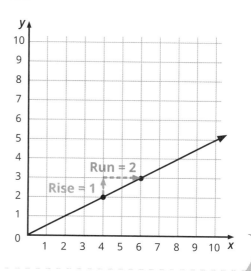

Find the slope of each proportional relationship.

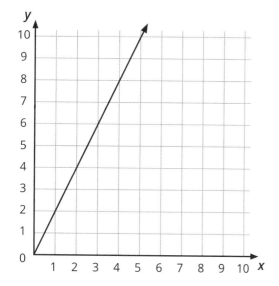

Slope = _____

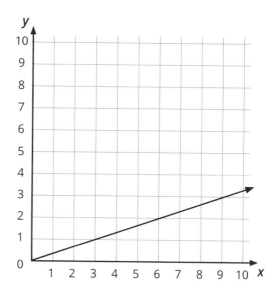

Slope = _____

Keep going! Find the slope of each proportional relationship.

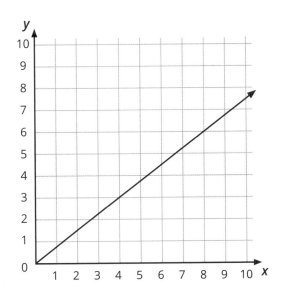

Slope = _____

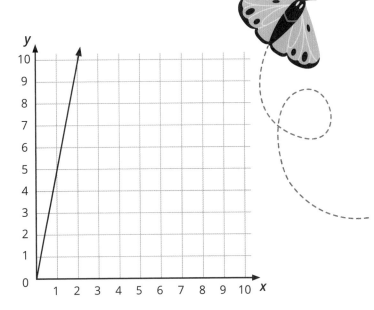

Slope = _____

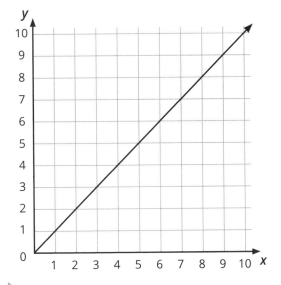

Slope = _____

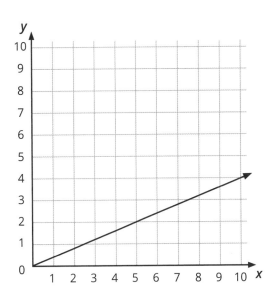

Slope = _____

KEEP IT GOING! Find the constant of proportionality for a few of the graphs on this page and the previous page. What do you notice about the relationship between the constant of proportionality and the slope?

In a proportional relationship, the constant of proportionality is the same as the slope. Graph each proportional relationship. Then write the slope.

Jade works at Pepe's Pizza. Yesterday, she used 9 cups of sauce to make 18 large pizzas. The amount of sauce, y, is proportional to the number of large pizzas, x.

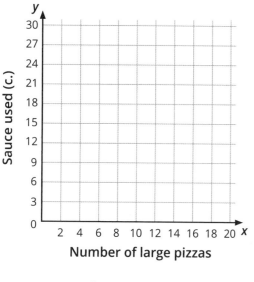

Slope = _____

At Ace Bowling Center, Lin paid $12 to play 4 games. The cost, y, is proportional to the number of games, x.

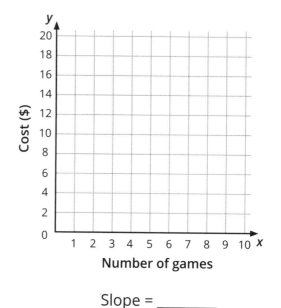

Slope = _____

Harry is making green paint for a mural. He mixes 2 gallons of blue paint and 5 gallons of yellow paint. The amount of blue paint, y, is proportional to the amount of yellow paint, x.

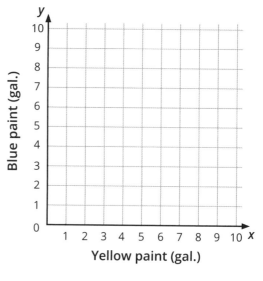

Slope = _____

Learn!

When you graph a linear relationship, the slope can be positive, negative, zero, or undefined.

Positive slope

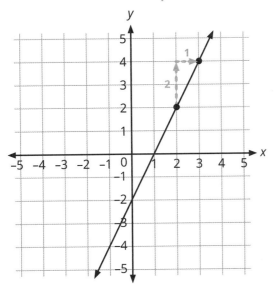

Lines with positive slopes rise from left to right.

$$\frac{\text{rise}}{\text{run}} = \frac{2}{1} = 2$$

Negative slope

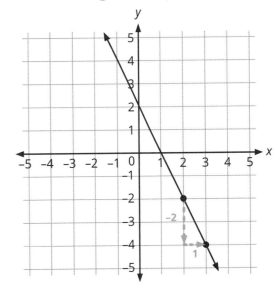

Lines with negative slopes fall from left to right.

$$\frac{\text{rise}}{\text{run}} = \frac{-2}{1} = -2$$

Zero slope

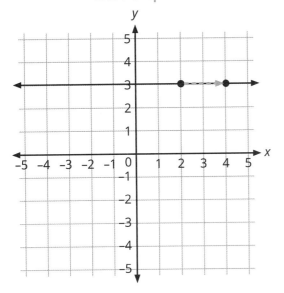

Lines with slopes of 0 are horizontal.

$$\frac{\text{rise}}{\text{run}} = \frac{0}{2} = 0$$

Undefined slope

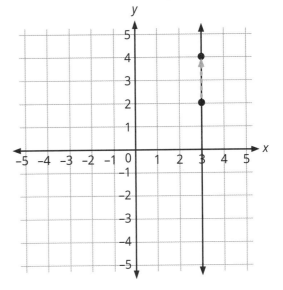

Lines with undefined slopes are vertical.

$$\frac{\text{rise}}{\text{run}} = \frac{2}{0} \qquad \frac{2}{0} \text{ is undefined.}$$

Determine which type of slope each line has. If the slope is positive or negative, write the value of the slope.

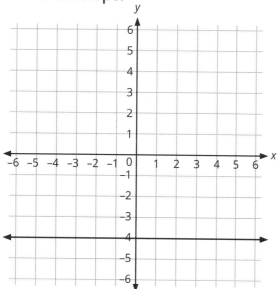

positive   negative   zero   undefined

Slope = _____

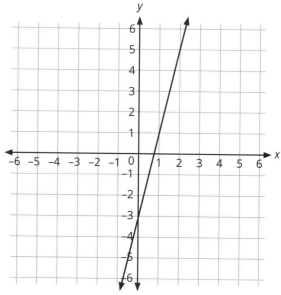

positive   negative   zero   undefined

Slope = _____

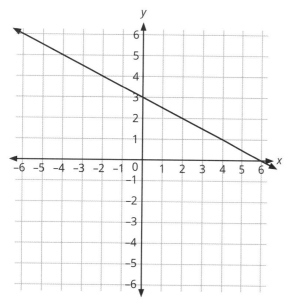

positive   negative   zero   undefined

Slope = _____

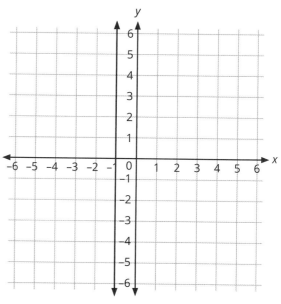

positive   negative   zero   undefined

Slope = _____

Graph each line described below.

a line with a slope of 2 that passes
through the point (0, 0)

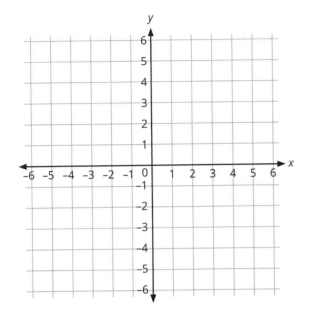

a line with a slope of 0 that passes
through the point (4, –1)

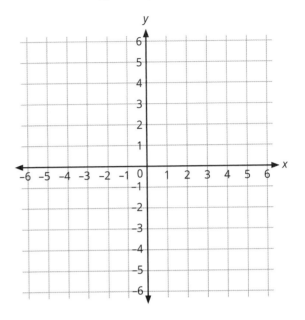

a line with a slope of $-\frac{3}{4}$ that passes
through the point (–4, 0)

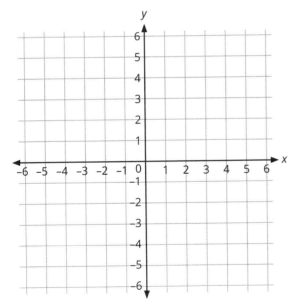

a line with a slope of $\frac{1}{3}$ that passes
through the point (–4, –3)

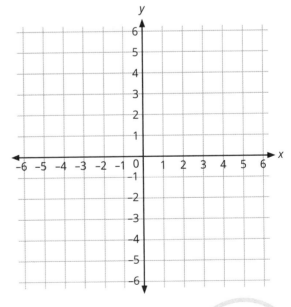

IXL.com
skill ID
FSV

Learn!

Slope is often represented using the variable m. Remember, slope is the ratio of the change in y to the change in x. You can find the slope of a line that passes through the points (x_1, y_1) and (x_2, y_2) using the formula below.

$$m = \frac{\text{change in } y}{\text{change in } x} = \frac{y_2 - y_1}{x_2 - x_1}$$

Try it! Find the slope of the line that passes through the points $(-5, -2)$ and $(1, 6)$.

Let $(-5, -2)$ be (x_1, y_1). Let $(1, 6)$ be (x_2, y_2). Plug the coordinates into the formula and simplify. Remember to write the slope as a simplified fraction or integer.

$$m = \frac{y_2 - y_1}{x_2 - x_1} = \frac{6 - (-2)}{1 - (-5)} = \frac{8}{6} = \frac{4}{3}$$

So, the slope of the line that passes through these two points is $\frac{4}{3}$.

Find the slope of the line that goes through each pair of points.

$(0, 4)$ and $(1, 2)$ $(3, 1)$ and $(4, 6)$ $(5, 2)$ and $(-10, 2)$

$m =$ _____ $m =$ _____ $m =$ _____

$(6, 0)$ and $(10, 2)$ $(-4, 4)$ and $(-3, 0)$ $(2, -1)$ and $(8, -5)$

$m =$ _____ $m =$ _____ $m =$ _____

IXL.com
skill ID
ZAC

Keep going! Find the slope of the line that goes through each pair of points.

(–5, 0) and (–4, 3)

(–3, –3) and (–11, –5)

(6, 4) and (8, –2)

m = _____

m = _____

m = _____

(0, –7) and (–3, –6)

(–10, –8) and (–8, 8)

(12, 20) and (15, 24)

m = _____

m = _____

m = _____

(–15, 5) and (–9, –16)

(–11, 16) and (–9, 2)

(–9, –13) and (–4, –10)

m = _____

m = _____

m = _____

(–12, –10) and (–9, 2)

(–1, 19) and (5, 11)

(–20, –2) and (–4, –20)

m = _____

m = _____

m = _____

Read the description of each line. Then write the ordered pair. Use the formula for slope to help you.

A line with a slope of –1 passes through the point (2, 7). Write the ordered pair of the point that lies on that line and has an *x*-coordinate of 6.

(_____ , _____)

A line with a slope of $\frac{1}{2}$ passes through the point (6, –2). Write the ordered pair of the point that lies on that line and has an *x*-coordinate of 2.

(_____ , _____)

A line with a slope of 2 passes through the point (5, 3). Write the ordered pair of the point that lies on that line and has a *y*-coordinate of –7.

(_____ , _____)

A line with a slope of $-\frac{3}{4}$ passes through the point (–9, 0). Write the ordered pair of the point that lies on that line and has a *y*-coordinate of –6.

(_____ , _____)

IXL.com
skill ID
R5P

Learn!

The **y-intercept** of a line is the *y*-coordinate of the point where the line crosses the *y*-axis. You can also think of the *y*-intercept as the value of *y* when *x* is equal to 0. It is often represented using the variable *b*.

Try it! Find the *y*-intercept of the line.

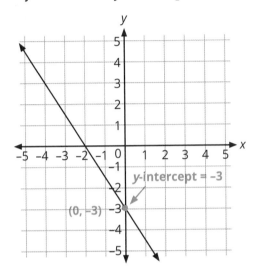

The line crosses the *y*-axis at the point (0, −3).

So, the *y*-intercept of the line is **−3**. You can also write this as *b* = **−3**.

Find the *y*-intercept of each line.

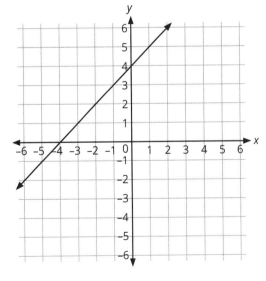

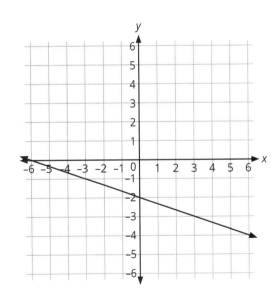

b = _____

b = _____

KEEP IT GOING! Find the slopes of the two lines in the problems above.

Learn!

Linear equations can be written in **slope-intercept form**:

$$y = mx + b$$

slope   y-intercept

Identify the slope and the *y*-intercept of each line.

$y = -2x + 5$	$y = \frac{1}{3}x + 8$	$y = 4x - 3$
$m = \underline{} -2$	$m = \underline{}$	$m = \underline{}$
$b = \underline{} 5$	$b = \underline{}$	$b = \underline{}$
$y = -\frac{1}{2}x - 1$	$y = 2 + 3x$	$y = 6 - x$
$m = \underline{}$	$m = \underline{}$	$m = \underline{}$
$b = \underline{}$	$b = \underline{}$	$b = \underline{}$

Write an equation in slope-intercept form for each line described below.

A line has a slope of 2 and a *y*-intercept of 4.

_____

A line has a slope of –3 and a *y*-intercept of 1.

_____

A line has a slope of $\frac{2}{3}$ and a *y*-intercept of –7.

_____

A line has a *y*-intercept of 0 and a slope of $\frac{4}{3}$.

_____

A line has a *y*-intercept of –2 and a slope of 1.

_____

Learn!

If you have a graph of a line, you can write its equation in slope-intercept form.

Try it! Write an equation in slope-intercept form for this line.

Start by identifying the slope, *m*, and the *y*-intercept, *b*.

$$m = \frac{\text{rise}}{\text{run}} = \frac{2}{4} = \frac{1}{2}$$

$$b = -2$$

Then, write the equation in the form **y = mx + b**.
Rewrite the equation using subtraction, if needed.

$$y = \frac{1}{2}x + (-2)$$

$$y = \frac{1}{2}x - 2$$

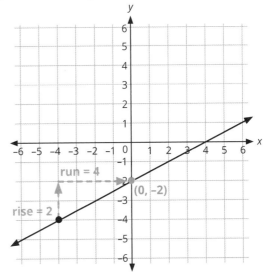

Identify the slope and *y*-intercept of each line. Then write an equation in slope-intercept form.

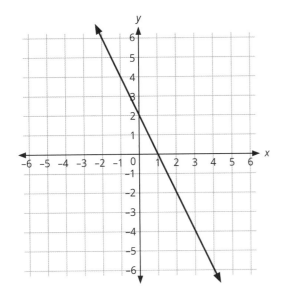

m = _____   *b* = _____

Equation: _____

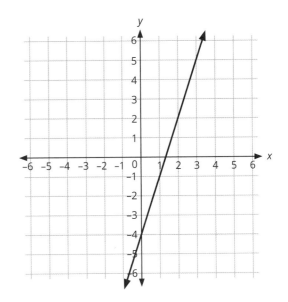

m = _____   *b* = _____

Equation: _____

Write an equation for each line in slope-intercept form.

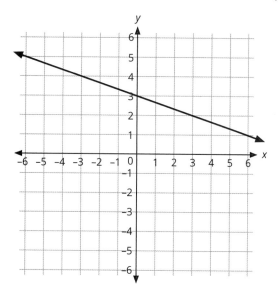

Equation: _____

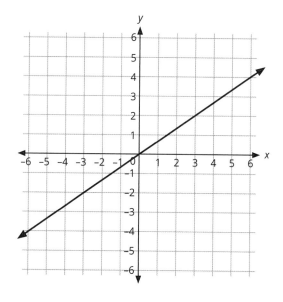

Equation: _____

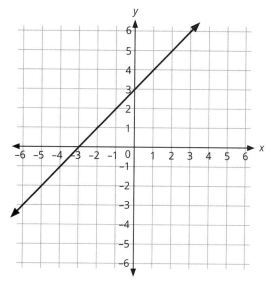

Equation: _____

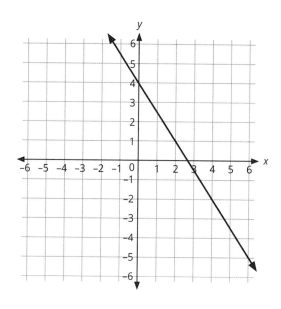

Equation: _____

IXL.com
skill ID
WHM

For more practice, visit IXL.com or the IXL mobile app and enter this code in the search bar.

Learn!

If you have an equation in slope-intercept form, you can use the slope and y-intercept to graph the line.

Try it! Graph $y = \frac{1}{3}x + 2$.

The slope of the line is $\frac{1}{3}$ and the y-intercept is 2.

Start by plotting the y-intercept on the graph. Place a point at (0, 2).

Then, use the slope to plot more points on the line. From the y-intercept, go up 1 and right 3 to plot another point on the line. You can also go in the opposite direction. Go down 1 and left 3 to plot another point on the line.

Finally, draw the line that connects the points.

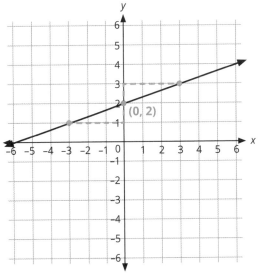

For each equation, write the slope and y-intercept. Then, graph the line.

$y = 2x - 3$ $m = $ _____

$b = $ _____

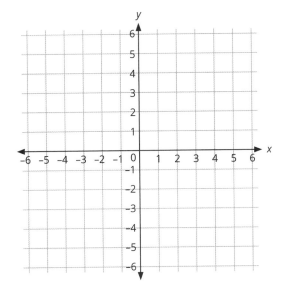

$y = -\frac{1}{4}x + 1$ $m = $ _____

$b = $ _____

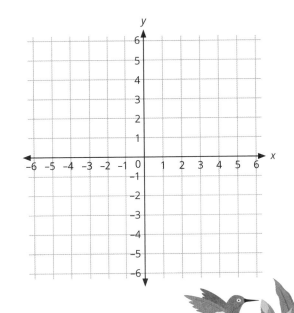

Graph each line.

$y = -3x + 4$

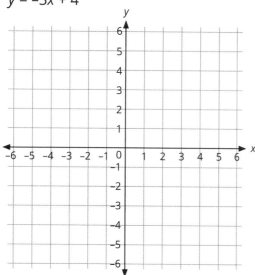

$y = \dfrac{5}{2}x - 2$

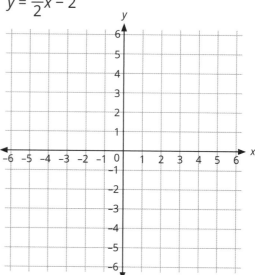

$y = \dfrac{2}{3}x + 1$

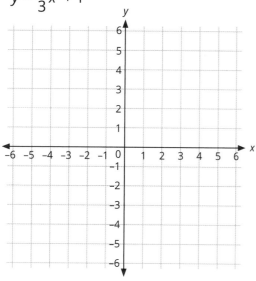

$y = -x + 3$

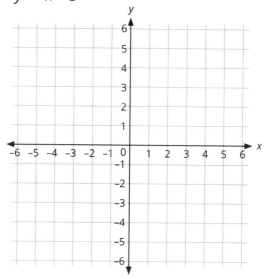

IXL.com
skill ID
W5E

If you have an equation that is not in slope-intercept form, you can rewrite the equation to help you graph the line.

Try it! Graph $3x - 4y = 8$.

First, solve the equation for y to put it in slope-intercept form.

$$3x - 4y = 8$$

$$-4y = -3x + 8$$

$$y = \frac{-3}{-4}x + \frac{8}{-4}$$

$$y = \frac{3}{4}x - 2$$

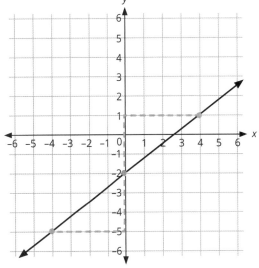

Now, graph the line. The slope of the line is $\frac{3}{4}$ and the y-intercept is -2.

Graph each line.

$5x - y = 4$

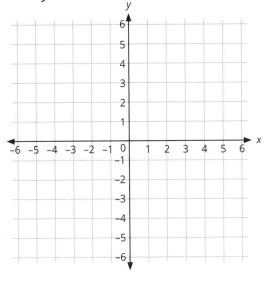

$x - 4y = 12$

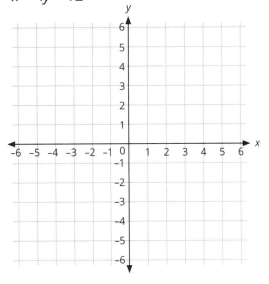

IXL.com
skill ID
7MZ

Keep going! Graph each line.

$2x + 3y = 9$

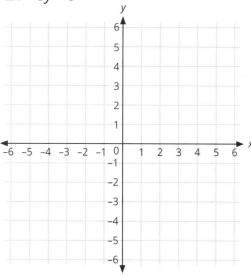

$3x + 2y = -6$

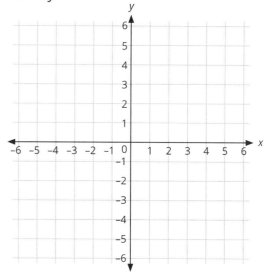

$4x + 3y = 6$

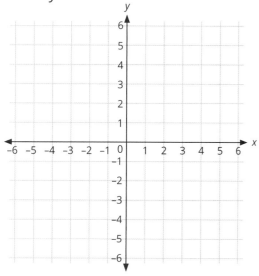

$x - 4y = 0$

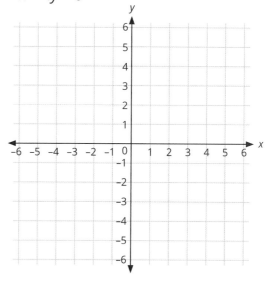

Learn!

The slope of a horizontal line is 0. Equations for horizontal lines can be written as **y = b**, where b is the y-intercept.

For example, this is the graph of $y = -2$. Every point on the line has a y-coordinate of –2.

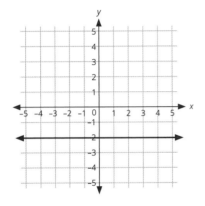

The slope of a vertical line is undefined. Equations for vertical lines can be written as **x = a**, where a is the x-intercept.

For example, this is the graph of $x = 3$. Every point on the line has an x-coordinate of 3.

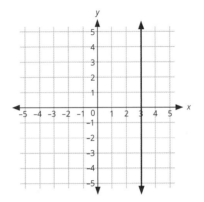

Graph each line.

$y = 1$

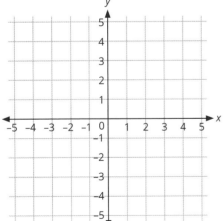

$x = -4$

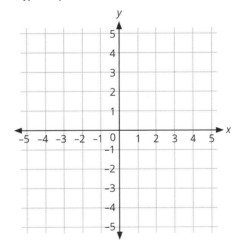

IXL.com
skill ID

ZWP

Learn!

When a table shows a linear relationship, you can write the relationship as an equation in slope-intercept form. Try it using the table below.

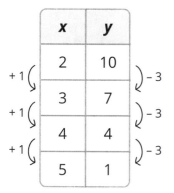

x	y
2	10
3	7
4	4
5	1

+ 1) – 3
+ 1) – 3
+ 1) – 3

First, find the **slope**. To do this, use the table to find the change in y and change in x. Then, divide.

$$m = \frac{\text{change in } y}{\text{change in } x}$$

$$m = \frac{-3}{1} = -3$$

So, the slope is -3.

Next, find the **y-intercept**, which is the y-value when $x = 0$. If the table does not include $x = 0$, you can use another row to solve for b.

$y = -3x + b$ Plug in the slope you found for m.

$10 = -3(2) + b$ Plug in the x- and y-values from any row of the table.

$10 = -6 + b$ Solve for b.

$16 = b$ So, the y-intercept is **16**.

Last, write the equation in slope-intercept form: $y = -3x + 16$.

Write an equation in slope-intercept form to represent the relationship in each table.

x	y
0	9
1	11
2	13

Equation: _____

x	y
0	24
2	16
4	8

Equation: _____

x	y
2	4
4	5
6	6

Equation: _____

x	y
1	–3
2	–1
3	1

Equation: _____

Keep going! Write an equation in slope-intercept form to represent the relationship in each table.

x	y
3	–8
4	–4
5	0

Equation: _____

x	y
5	4
10	7
15	10

Equation: _____

x	y
10	10
13	7
16	4

Equation: _____

x	y
5	0
7	–6
9	–12

Equation: _____

x	y
4	–9
8	–8
12	–7

Equation: _____

x	y
6	–4
9	–8
12	–12

Equation: _____

Learn!

If you know the slope of a line and a point on the line, you can write the equation of the line in slope-intercept form.

Try writing the equation of the line that has a slope of −4 and goes through the point (2, −10). Plug the values you know into $y = mx + b$ and solve for b.

$y = -4x + b$	Plug in the slope for m.
$-10 = -4(2) + b$	Plug in the known coordinates for x and y.
$-10 = -8 + b$	Solve for b.
$-2 = b$	So, the y-intercept is −2.

Now, write the equation in slope-intercept form: $y = -4x - 2$.

In each problem, you are given the slope of a line and a point on that line. Write the equation of each line in slope-intercept form.

$m = 5$
Point: (3, 9)

Equation: _____

$m = -2$
Point: (4, −4)

Equation: _____

$m = \dfrac{3}{4}$
Point: (−8, −3)

Equation: _____

$m = -\dfrac{5}{2}$
Point: (10, −20)

Equation: _____

You can also write the equation of a line if you know the *y*-intercept and a point on the line. Plug the values you know into $y = mx + b$ and solve for *m*. Then write the equation of the line in slope-intercept form.

$b = 7$

Point: (10, –3)

$$y = mx + 7$$
$$-3 = m(10) + 7$$
$$-3 = 10m + 7$$
$$-10 = 10m$$
$$-1 = m$$

Equation: $\underline{\quad y = -x + 7 \quad}$

$b = 2$

Point: (5, 4)

Equation: _____

$b = -8$

Point: (–2, –14)

Equation: _____

$b = -3$

Point: (–12, 3)

Equation: _____

In each problem below, you are given either the slope or the *y*-intercept of a line and a point on the line. Write the equation of each line in slope-intercept form.

$m = -8$

Point: (3, –16)

Equation: _____

$b = -30$

Point: (40, –2)

Equation: _____

$b = 5$

Point: (12, –3)

Equation: _____

$m = -4$

Point: (8, –20)

Equation: _____

Learn!

If you know any two points on a line, you can write the equation of the line in slope-intercept form.

Try writing the equation of the line that goes through the points $(-1, -5)$ and $(2, 7)$.

First, find the **slope** between the two points using the slope formula:

$$m = \frac{y_2 - y_1}{x_2 - x_1}$$

$$m = \frac{7 - (-5)}{2 - (-1)} = \frac{12}{3} = 4$$

So, the slope is 4.

Next, find the *y*-intercept.

$y = 4x + b$ Plug in the slope you found.

$7 = 4(2) + b$ Plug in the *x*- and *y*-values from either one of the points.

$7 = 8 + b$ Solve for *b*.

$-1 = b$ So, the *y*-intercept is -1.

Last, write the equation in slope-intercept form: $y = 4x - 1$.

In each problem, you are given two points that fall on a line. Write the equation of each line in slope-intercept form.

$(2, 4)$ and $(4, 20)$

Equation: _____

$(3, 0)$ and $(1, 4)$

Equation: _____

$(-4, 3)$ and $(8, 6)$

Equation: _____

$(-9, -4)$ and $(6, -9)$

Equation: _____

Keep going! Write the equation of each line in slope-intercept form.

(10, 0) and (–5, –3)

Equation: _____

(–2, –9) and (4, 21)

Equation: _____

(3, 12) and (–3, –24)

Equation: _____

(16, 6) and (8, –1)

Equation: _____

(5, 8) and (10, 8)

Equation: _____

(–1, –2) and (–7, 4)

Equation: _____

(2, –13) and (1, –5)

Equation: _____

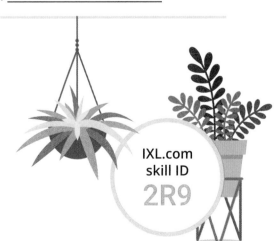

IXL.com
skill ID
2R9

Learn!

You can identify parallel and perpendicular lines based on their slopes.

Parallel lines have the same slope.

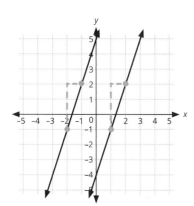

$y = 3x + 5$

$y = 3x - 4$

Both lines have a slope of 3.

Perpendicular lines have opposite reciprocal slopes.

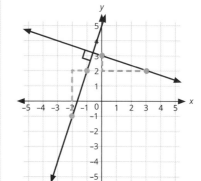

$y = 3x + 5$

$y = -\dfrac{1}{3}x + 3$

The slopes 3 and $-\dfrac{1}{3}$ have opposite signs, and $\dfrac{3}{1}$ and $\dfrac{1}{3}$ are reciprocals.

Find the slope of a line that is either parallel or perpendicular to the line shown on each graph.

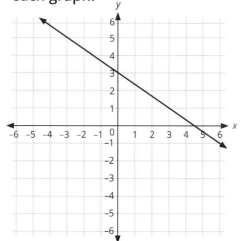

Slope of a parallel line = _____

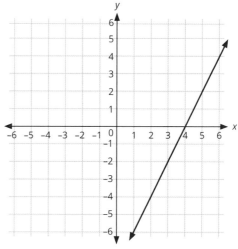

Slope of a perpendicular line = _____

IXL.com
skill ID
PRP

Find the slope of a line that is either parallel or perpendicular to the line represented by the equation.

$y = -4x - 5$ Slope of a parallel line = _____

$y = -\dfrac{2}{5}x + 6$ Slope of a perpendicular line = _____

Find the slope of a line that is either parallel or perpendicular to the line going through the two given points.

(–2, –4) and (3, –3)

Slope of a perpendicular line = _____

(9, 0) and (4, –3)

Slope of a parallel line = _____

(–8, –9) and (0, –13)

Slope of a parallel line = _____

(10, 12) and (4, 10)

Slope of a perpendicular line = _____

Write an equation in slope-intercept form for each line.

The line through (–6, 2) that is parallel to $y = \frac{1}{3}x - 5$

Equation: _____

The line through (–12, –1) that is perpendicular to $y = -6x + 2$

Equation: _____

Fill in the blanks to answer each question.

Javier decides to join his neighborhood gym. He pays a one-time joining fee as well as a monthly membership fee. This situation can be modeled as a linear relationship.

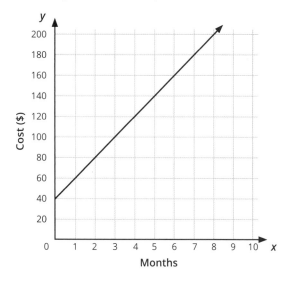

What does the *y*-intercept of the line tell you about the situation?

The one-time joining fee is $ _____.

What does the slope of the line tell you about the situation?

The monthly membership fee is $ _____.

Write an equation relating the total cost, *y*, to the number of months Javier holds his gym membership, *x*.

$y =$ _____ $x +$ _____

Quinn has a basket of cayenne peppers that she is using to make hot sauce. She uses the same number of cayenne peppers for each jar of hot sauce. This situation can be modeled as a linear relationship.

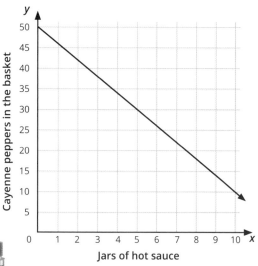

What does the *y*-intercept of the line tell you about the situation?

Quinn started with _____ cayenne peppers in the basket.

What does the slope of the line tell you about the situation?

Quinn uses _____ cayenne peppers for every jar of hot sauce she makes.

Write an equation relating the number of cayenne peppers in the basket, *y*, to the number of jars of hot sauce Quinn makes, *x*.

$y =$ _____ $x +$ _____

Write a linear equation in slope-intercept form to represent each problem.

Chelsea is making mugs in a pottery studio. She can make 4 mugs with the clay that she already has in the studio. She can make 12 additional mugs with each bag of clay she purchases. Write an equation that shows how the total number of mugs Chelsea can make, y, depends on the number of bags of clay she purchases, x.

_____

Jenaya loaded her subway pass with $40. Each time she rides the subway, $1.50 is deducted from her pass. Write an equation that shows the relationship between the number of times Jenaya rides the subway, x, and the amount of money left on her subway pass, y.

_____

Drake decides to save $10 per week starting in the new year. He already has $45 saved at the beginning of the year. Write an equation to show how the amount of money Drake has saved, y, depends on the number of weeks that have passed, x.

_____

Rose enjoys launching her model rocket. After the parachute deploys, the rocket descends at a constant rate of 4 meters per second. In today's launch, the parachute deployed at an altitude of 350 meters. Write an equation that shows the relationship between the number of seconds since the parachute was deployed, x, and the altitude of the model rocket, y.

_____

Speedy Moving Company rents cargo vans to customers. For a one-day rental, they charge a $30 flat rate and an additional $0.75 per mile. Write an equation that shows how the cost, y, depends on the number of miles driven, x.

_____

Elijah's family is going to the Westport County Fair. For each problem below, write a linear equation in slope-intercept form. Then answer each question.

When Elijah's family arrives at the Westport County Fair, they pay $15 admission per person plus $5 to park their car. Write an equation that shows how the total cost, y, depends on the number of people in Elijah's family, x.

Equation: _____

If there are 4 people in Elijah's family, what is the total cost of parking and admission?

_____

Each ride costs 3 tickets. Elijah has 36 tickets. Write an equation that relates the number of rides Elijah goes on, x, to the number of tickets remaining, y.

Equation: _____

What is the greatest number of rides Elijah can go on with the tickets he has?

_____

There is a long line for the Ferris wheel. Elijah is standing 28 feet from the front of the line. Each minute, he moves 2 feet closer. Write an equation that shows how Elijah's distance from the front of the line, y, depends on the number of minutes he waits, x.

Equation: _____

How many minutes will it take Elijah to reach the front of the line?

_____

Elijah has $20 to spend on lunch at the food trucks. Elijah buys hot dogs, which cost $4.50 each. Write an equation that relates the number of hot dogs Elijah buys, x, to the amount of money he has left, y.

Equation: _____

If Elijah has $11 left, how many hot dogs did he buy?

_____

IXL.com
skill ID
DA6

Answer each question.

Chloe wants to book a DJ for her graduation party. The DJ charges an initial booking fee as well as an hourly rate. If Chloe books the DJ for 3 hours, it will cost $135. If she books the DJ for 5 hours, it will cost $175.

What is the DJ's hourly rate?	What is the DJ's initial booking fee?
Write an equation that shows how the total cost, y, depends on the number of hours the DJ is booked, x.	If Chloe wants to spend $155, how many hours can she book the DJ for?

Mateo works at a bakery. He buys a large bag of flour to make bread. After Mateo has made 8 loaves, there are 48 pounds of flour left in the bag. After he has made 40 loaves, there are 40 pounds of flour left.

How many pounds of flour does Mateo use for each loaf of bread?	When the bag was full, how many pounds of flour did it hold?
Write an equation that shows how the number of pounds of flour left in the bag, y, depends on the number of loaves of bread Mateo makes, x.	How many pounds of flour will be left in the bag after Mateo makes 100 loaves of bread?

Learn!

Two linear equations that use the same variables form a **system of linear equations**. A solution to a system of linear equations is a point where the lines intersect. The coordinates of that point make both equations true. Systems of linear equations can have one solution, no solution, or infinitely many solutions.

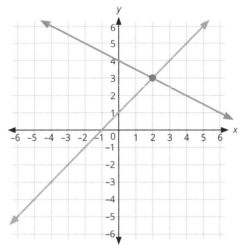

If the lines intersect at exactly one point, then the system has exactly **one solution**. This happens when the slopes of the lines are different, like with this system.

So, this system has one solution.
$$y = x + 1$$
$$y = -\frac{1}{2}x + 4$$

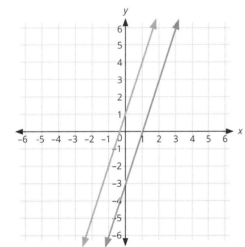

If the lines never intersect, then the system has **no solution**. This happens when the lines are parallel, like with this system. Parallel lines have the same slope but different y-intercepts.

So, this system has no solution.
$$y = 3x + 1$$
$$y = 3x - 3$$

If the lines intersect at every point, then the system has **infinitely many solutions**. This happens when the equations represent the same line, like with this system.

So, this system has infinitely many solutions.
$$y = 2x - 2$$
$$-2x + y = -2$$

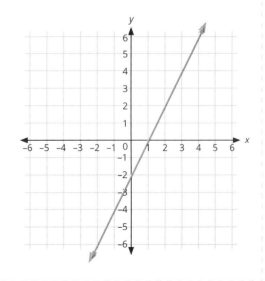

Notice that $-2x + y = -2$ can be written as $y = 2x - 2$.

Determine whether each system of equations has one solution, no solution, or infinitely many solutions.

$y = 4x + 3$ $y = 3x + 4$	one solution	$y = 2 - \dfrac{2}{3}x$ $y = -\dfrac{2}{3}x + 2$	
$y = 6x + 2$ $-6x + y = 4$		$y = -\dfrac{1}{2}x - 1$ $-10y = 5x + 10$	
$y = 5 - 2x$ $y = -\dfrac{3}{5}x - 2$		$2y = 6x - 12$ $3x - y = 2$	
$x - y = -3$ $-\dfrac{1}{3}x + \dfrac{1}{3}y = 1$		$3y = 12x + 15$ $4x + y = 5$	
$8x - y = 5$ $-8x + y = 11$		$-\dfrac{3}{4}x - y = -3$ $4y = 12 - 3x$	

SEE FOR YOURSELF! The point (1, 7) is the solution to the first problem on the page. Try plugging $x = 1$ and $y = 7$ into both equations. Are they both true?

IXL.com
skill ID

UYM

Learn!

You can solve a system of linear equations by graphing the lines and finding the point of intersection. Try it! Solve the system of equations below by graphing.

$$y = 3x - 2 \qquad y = -\frac{1}{2}x + 5$$

To help graph the equations, make sure each equation is written in slope-intercept form. Here, both equations are in slope-intercept form.

Graph each equation in the system and find the point of intersection.

The point of intersection, (2, 4), is the solution to the system.

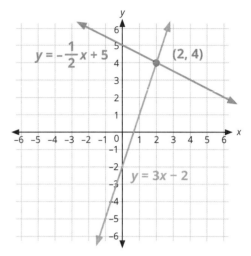

Solve each system of equations by graphing. Then write the solution.

$$y = -x + 4 \qquad y = 2x - 5$$

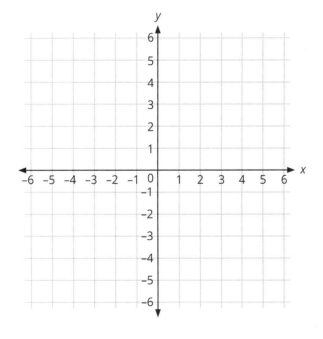

Solution: (_____ , _____)

$$y = x - 1 \qquad y = 3x + 5$$

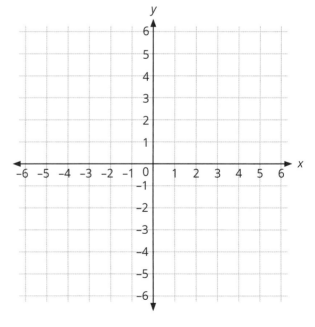

Solution: (_____ , _____)

Keep going! Solve each system of equations by graphing. Then write the solution.

$y = \dfrac{1}{2}x - 2$ $y = -\dfrac{1}{4}x + 1$

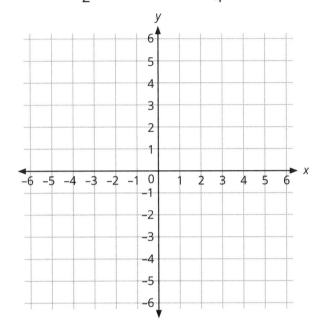

Solution: (_____ , _____)

$2y = x + 6$ $x + y = -3$

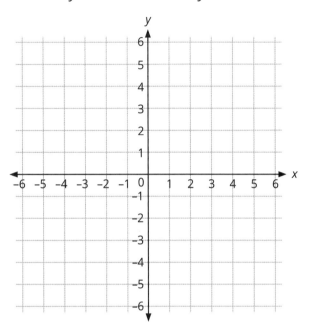

Solution: (_____ , _____)

$3y = 9 - 3x$ $y = \dfrac{2}{3}x - 2$

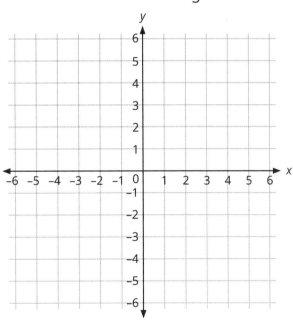

Solution: (_____ , _____)

Learn!

Another method you can use to solve systems of linear equations is called **substitution**. Follow the steps below to learn how.

To use substitution, one of the equations needs to be written so that a variable is isolated. In this system, neither equation has a variable that is isolated.

$$x + 2y = 2$$
$$-2x + y = 6$$

Select an equation and isolate either x or y. Choose the equation and variable you think would be easier to isolate. Here, take $-2x + y = 6$ and isolate y.

$$-2x + y = 6$$
$$y = 2x + 6$$

Since $y = 2x + 6$, you can substitute $2x + 6$ for y in the other equation, $x + 2y = 2$. Then solve for x.

$$x + 2y = 2$$
$$x + 2(2x + 6) = 2$$
$$x + 4x + 12 = 2$$
$$5x + 12 = 2$$
$$5x = -10$$
$$x = -2$$

Now that you know $x = -2$, you can find y. Substitute -2 for x in either equation and solve for y. Here, use the equation $x + 2y = 2$.

$$x + 2y = 2$$
$$-2 + 2y = 2$$
$$2y = 4$$
$$y = 2$$

Since $x = -2$ and $y = 2$, the solution to the system of equations is $(-2, 2)$.

Solve each system of equations using substitution.

$$y = -x + 3$$
$$y = 2x$$

$$x = -4$$
$$y = \frac{1}{2}x + 3$$

(_____ , _____)

(_____ , _____)

Keep going! Solve each system of equations using substitution.

$3x + y = 12$

$-5x + y = -4$

(_____ , _____)

$3x - 4y = 4$

$-4x + y = 12$

(_____ , _____)

$-y = 8 + x$

$2y = 6x + 8$

(_____ , _____)

$4x + y = 2$

$3y = 3x - 24$

(_____ , _____)

$2x + y = 6$

$-5x + y = -8$

(_____ , _____)

$10y = 9x + 30$

$12x + y = 3$

(_____ , _____)

Another method you can use to solve systems of linear equations is called **elimination**. Follow the steps below to learn how.

To use elimination, the equations need to be written so that you can add or subtract them to eliminate a variable term. In other words, the coefficients of one of the variables need to be either the same or opposite numbers. In this system, neither variable has coefficients that are the same or opposite numbers.

$$x + y = 6$$
$$3x - 2y = 8$$

Rewrite the equations to help you eliminate a variable term. Here, rewrite $x + y = 6$ so that the coefficient of y is 2. To do this, multiply both sides of the equation by 2 so that the two sides of the equation are still equal. This will allow you to eliminate the y term when you add the equations.

$$x + y = 6$$
$$(2)(x + y) = (2)(6)$$
$$2x + 2y = 12$$

Add or subtract the equations to eliminate a variable. Here, since $+2$ and -2 are opposite coefficients, you can add the two equations to eliminate y. Then solve for x.

$$2x + 2y = 12$$
$$+\ 3x - 2y = 8$$
$$\overline{5x + 0y = 20}$$
$$5x = 20$$
$$x = 4$$

Now that you know the value of x, you can use it to find y. Substitute 4 for x in either equation to solve for y. Here, use $x + y = 6$.

$$x + y = 6$$
$$4 + y = 6$$
$$y = 2$$

Since $x = 4$ and $y = 2$, the solution to the system of equations is (4, 2).

Solve each system of equations using elimination.

$x + 2y = 5$
$-x + y = 4$

$-3x + 6y = 6$
$3x - y = 4$

(_____ , _____)

(_____ , _____)

Keep going! Solve each system of equations using elimination.

$4x - 2y = -2$
$-4x + 4y = 12$

(____ , ____)

$2x + 7y = -13$
$2x + y = -7$

(____ , ____)

$2x + y = 1$
$-x + 2y = -8$

(____ , ____)

$3x + 2y = 20$
$2x + 4y = 24$

(____ , ____)

$2x + 2y = 8$
$4x + 3y = 12$

(____ , ____)

$-8x + 2y = -12$
$-6x + 3y = -6$

(____ , ____)

$12x + 3y = 9$
$-5x + 2y = -20$

(____ , ____)

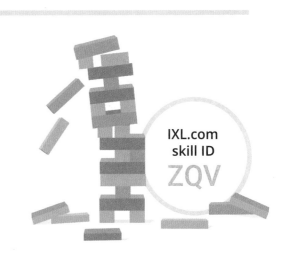

IXL.com
skill ID
ZQV

Solve each system of equations using any method.

$3x - y = 4$
$y = 8 - x$

(_____ , _____)

$2x + 4y = -8$
$-3x + y = 12$

(_____ , _____)

$y = x - 5$
$3x + 2y = -20$

(_____ , _____)

$-4x + y = -5$
$4x + y = 3$

(_____ , _____)

$-4x - 2y = 6$
$10x + 2y = 12$

(_____ , _____)

$-x + 2y = 14$
$3x + 4y = 8$

(_____ , _____)

IXL.com
skill ID
AM5

$4x + y = -9$
$x + 4y = 24$

(_____ , _____)

Solve the systems of equations and look for places where that solution appears in the code. Use the code to reveal the rest of the joke! Not every letter will be used in the code at the bottom.

E	$y = \frac{3}{2}x + 1$ $x + 2y = 10$	**U**	$4x - y = 4$ $y = 3x - 1$
C	$x + y = -5$ $-x + y = 7$	**A**	$\frac{2}{5}x + y = -1$ $2x + y = 7$
D	$4x + 2y = 2$ $5x + y = -2$	**T**	$5x + 6y = 6$ $-4x + 3y = -36$
O	$-6x + 3y = -24$ $3x + 6y = 12$	**B**	$-2x + 8y = -16$ $6x + 4y = 20$

Why did the boy refuse to drink the glass of water with eight ice cubes in it?

It was _____ _____ _____   _____ _____ _____ _____ _____!

(6, –4) (4, 0) (4, 0)   (–6, 1) (3, 8) (4, –1) (2, 4) (–1, 3)

Write a system of equations to represent each scenario. Then solve the system of equations to answer the questions.

Lila and her sister Ava are saving up money to spend on vacation. Lila has $55 saved already, and she sets a goal to save an additional $10 each week. Ava has $65 saved already, and she sets a goal to save an additional $8 each week. If Lila and Ava each meet their savings goals, how many weeks will it take for them to have the same amount of money saved? How much money will they each have saved at that point?

Tamara is a baker at Rise and Shine Bakery. On Monday, Tamara uses 34 peaches to make 2 peach crisps and 3 peach pies. On Tuesday, she uses 28 peaches to make 4 peach crisps and 1 peach pie. How many peaches does Tamara use in each peach crisp? How many peaches does she use in each peach pie?

Kassim volunteers at Paw Pals Animal Rescue. Last month, he ordered 3 bags of cat food and 5 bags of dog food. The shipment of pet food weighed 290 pounds. This month, he ordered 2 bags of cat food and 6 bags of dog food. The shipment weighed 300 pounds. How much does each bag of cat food weigh? How much does each bag of dog food weigh?

The eighth-grade students at Brighton Middle School are going on a field trip to the aquarium. Write a system of equations to represent each scenario. Then solve the system of equations to answer the questions.

Admission to the aquarium costs $8 for each student and $12 for each chaperone. There are 120 people going on the field trip. If the total cost of admission is $1,020, how many students are on the field trip? How many chaperones are on the field trip?

The aquarium has two types of penguins: little blue penguins and Adélie penguins. There are 15 penguins in all. Each little blue penguin eats 2 kilograms of fish per day, and each Adélie penguin eats 3 kilograms of fish per day. In total, all of the penguins eat 39 kilograms of fish each day. How many of the penguins are little blue penguins? How many of the penguins are Adélie penguins?

During their visit, students got to choose between attending a sea lion show and watching a 3D movie. Admission to the sea lion show is $4. Admission to the movie is $3. The total cost of tickets for all 120 people on the trip was $449. How many people attended the sea lion show? How many people watched the 3D movie?

Challenge!

IXL.com
Checkpoint ID

MFL

A **relation** is a rule that assigns input values to output values. A relation is a **function** if every input value is assigned to exactly one output value. You can represent relations using ordered pairs, tables, and mapping diagrams. Look at the examples below.

Relation F:

Ordered pairs:

(1, 8), (5, 10), (6, 2), (8, 11)

Table:

x	y
1	8
5	10
6	2
8	11

Mapping diagram:

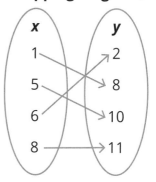

Relation F is a function because each input, or *x*-value, has exactly one output, or *y*-value.

Relation G:

Ordered pairs:

(2, 2), (2, 4), (3, 3), (5, 1)

Table:

x	y
2	2
2	4
3	3
5	1

Mapping diagram:

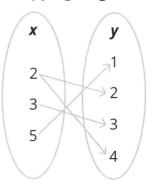

Relation G is **not** a function because the input value 2 has two different output values.

Determine if each relation is a function.

(–4, 0), (–3, 1), (–2, 0), (–2, –1)

function   not a function

(2, 1), (4, 1), (6, 2), (8, 3)

function   not a function

Keep going! Determine if each relation is a function.

x	y
5	−2
7	−5
9	1
11	−2

function   not a function

x	y
3	1
4	9
5	2
5	6

function   not a function

x	y
−2	2
−1	4
0	6
1	8

function   not a function

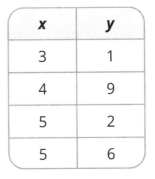

function   not a function

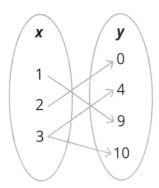

function   not a function

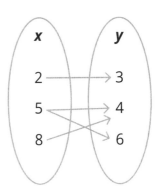

function   not a function

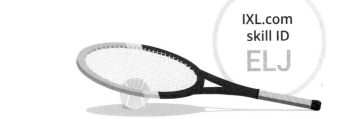

In each row below, the same incomplete relation is given twice. Follow the directions to make each relation either a function or not a function.

Add a new ordered pair to make a relation that is a function.

(18, 3), (15, –2), (12, –7), (_____ , _____)

Add a new ordered pair to make a relation that is **not** a function.

(18, 3), (15, –2), (12, –7), (_____ , _____)

Draw arrows to make a relation that is a function.

x	y
1	–3
2	–1
3	1
4	3

Draw arrows to make a relation that is **not** a function.

x	y
1	–3
2	–1
3	1
4	3

Complete the table to make a relation that is a function.

x	y
3	4
7	–2
15	3

Complete the table to make a relation that is **not** a function.

x	y
3	4
7	–2
15	3

Determine if each graph represents a function. Then explain your thinking.

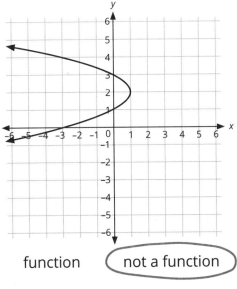

function   (not a function)

How do you know?

The x-value –2 has two different

y-values. So, this is not a function.

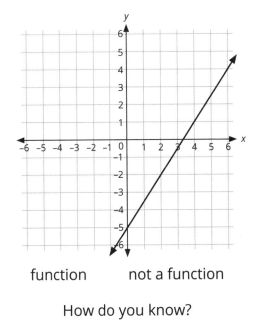

function   not a function

How do you know?

_____

_____

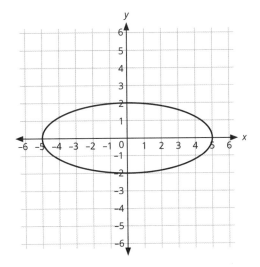

function   not a function

How do you know?

_____

_____

TAKE ANOTHER LOOK! If you draw vertical lines in the problems above, each line you draw will touch the graph exactly once if it represents a function. If any vertical line crosses the graph more than once, then the graph does not represent a function. Try this on the graphs above to check your answers!

IXL.com skill ID

AEB

Find the slope of each function. Then determine which function has the greater slope.

Function P

$y = 2x + 6$

Function Q

x	y
3	7
4	10
5	13

Function R

$3x - 4y = 9$

Function S

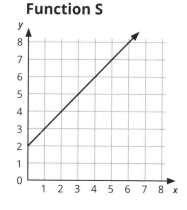

Slope = _____   Slope = _____

Slope = _____   Slope = _____

Which function has a greater slope?

_____

Which function has a greater slope?

_____

Function A

x	y
14	–3
16	2
18	7

Function B

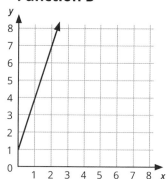

Slope = _____   Slope = _____

Which function has a greater slope?

_____

Find the *y*-intercept of each function. Then determine which function has the greater *y*-intercept.

Function T

x	y
6	10
8	13
10	16

Function U

$y = 2x + 3$

Function C

$y = \dfrac{2}{3}x + 1$

Function D

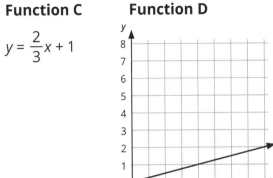

y-intercept = _____   *y*-intercept = _____

y-intercept = _____   *y*-intercept = _____

Which function has a greater *y*-intercept?

_____

Which function has a greater *y*-intercept?

_____

Function J

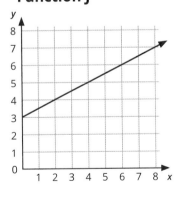

Function K

x	y
2	8
3	10
4	12

y-intercept = _____   *y*-intercept = _____

Which function has a greater *y*-intercept?

_____

Challenge!

IXL.com
Checkpoint ID

XQJ

Write a linear equation in slope-intercept form to represent each function.

Mason's older brother, Noah, wants to rent an electric scooter to get around the city. The graph of the line represents the cost of renting an electric scooter. Write a linear function to represent the total cost, c, of renting the electric scooter for t minutes.

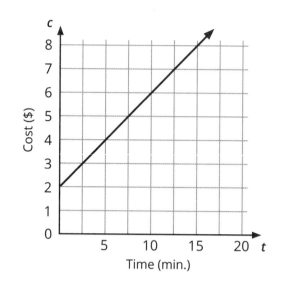

_____

Sondra is making cookies for a cookie exchange. The table represents the number of eggs remaining as she bakes. Write a linear function to represent the number of eggs remaining, g, after Sondra bakes b batches of cookies.

Batches baked	Eggs remaining
2	20
4	16
6	12
8	8

_____

Valeria and Mina are hiking. The graph of the line represents their elevation during the hike. Write a linear function to represent Valeria and Mina's elevation, h, after t hours.

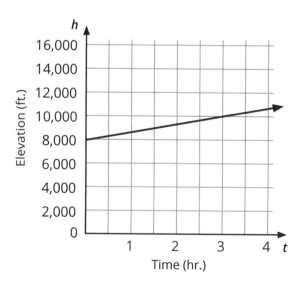

_____

Write a linear equation in slope-intercept form to represent each function. Then use the equation you wrote to answer the question.

Mr. Anderson is hiring a caterer for his mom's 90th birthday party. The table represents the total cost for catering. Write a linear function to represent the total cost, c, of getting catering for p people.

Number of people	Total cost ($)
10	180
20	310
30	440
40	570

_____

What is the cost for each additional person? _____

Mr. Garcia started a new job at a shipping warehouse. On his first paycheck, he will receive his hourly rate for the number of hours he works and a starting bonus. If he works 20 hours, he will receive $870 on his first paycheck. If he works 40 hours, he will receive $1,290 on his first paycheck. Write a linear function to represent the pay Mr. Garcia receives, p, based on Mr. Garcia working h hours.

_____

How much is Mr. Garcia's starting bonus? _____

Marco's cat, Luna, had kittens. The graph of the line represents the weight of the smallest kitten in the litter. Write a linear function to represent the kitten's weight, w, after t weeks.

_____

How many grams does the kitten gain each week?

_____

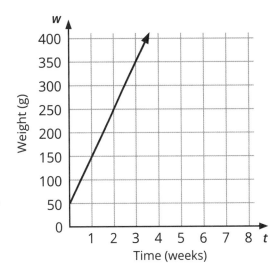

Learn!

Functions can be linear or nonlinear.

If a function has a constant rate of change, it is **linear**. The graph of a linear function is a straight line. Linear functions can be written in the form $y = mx + b$.

For example, $y = 3x - 2$ is a linear function.

If a function does not have a constant rate of change, it is **nonlinear**. The graph of a nonlinear function is not a straight line. Nonlinear functions cannot be written in the form $y = mx + b$.

For example, $y = x^2$ is a nonlinear function.

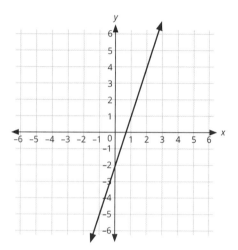

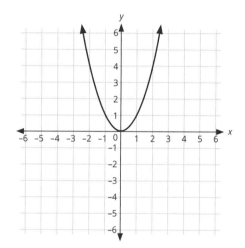

Determine whether each graph represents a linear function or a nonlinear function.

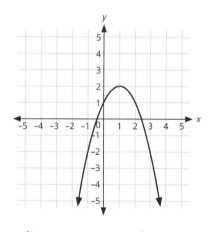

linear   nonlinear

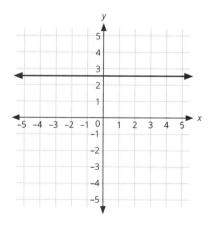

linear   nonlinear

Linear and nonlinear functions

Determine whether each equation represents a linear function or a nonlinear function.

$y = \frac{2}{3}x + 6$

linear nonlinear

$y = 3x^3 + 1$

linear nonlinear

$3x - y = 8$

linear nonlinear

Determine whether each table represents a linear function or a nonlinear function.

x	y
1	–13
2	–18
3	–23
4	–28

linear nonlinear

x	y
1	2
2	4
3	8
4	16

linear nonlinear

x	y
1	0
2	3
3	8
4	15

linear nonlinear

x	y
1	–1
2	–8
3	–27
4	–64

linear nonlinear

x	y
5	85
10	78
15	71
20	64

linear nonlinear

x	y
6	16
7	29
8	44
9	61

linear nonlinear

Challenge!

IXL.com
Checkpoint ID
JKA

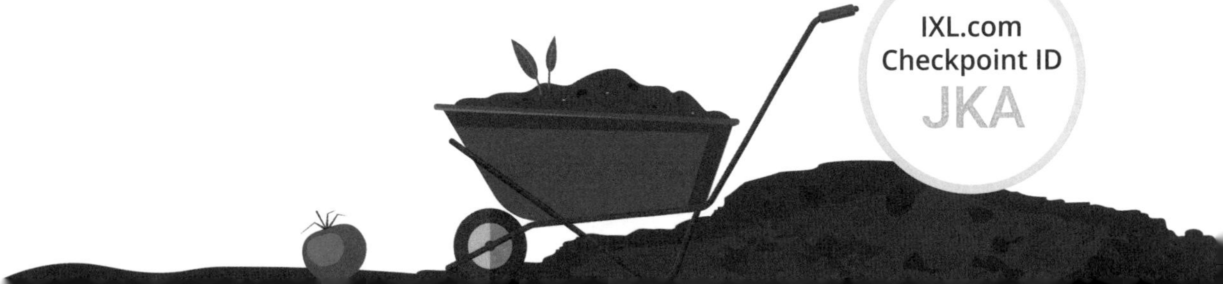

Exploration Zone

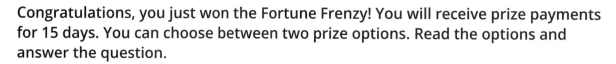

Congratulations, you just won the Fortune Frenzy! You will receive prize payments for 15 days. You can choose between two prize options. Read the options and answer the question.

Prize 1: Receive $1,000 every day.

Prize 2: Receive $2 on the first day and double the total prize amount each day after.

Which prize sounds more appealing? Why? _____

_____

Fill in the tables below to show how much money you would receive with each prize.

Prize 1	
Day	Total money
1	$1,000
2	$2,000
3	$3,000
4	
5	
6	
7	
8	
9	
10	
11	
12	
13	
14	
15	

Prize 2	
Day	Total money
1	$2
2	$4
3	$8
4	
5	
6	
7	
8	
9	
10	
11	
12	
13	
14	
15	

Answer the following questions based on the tables on the previous page.

On which days is the amount received from Prize 1 greater?   _____

On which days is the amount received from Prize 2 greater?   _____

Which prize represents a linear relationship?   _____

Model that prize using a linear function in the form $y = mx + b$,   _____
where x is the number of days and y is the total prize money.

The other table represents an exponential relationship. You can model that prize using the exponential function $y = 2^x$.

Using the tables from the previous page, graph the points for the even-numbered days for Prize 1 and Prize 2. Connect the points of the linear relationship with a line. Connect the points of the exponential relationship with a curve.

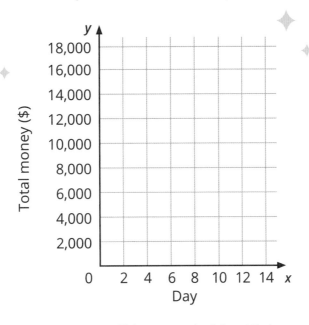

Knowing that the prize payments will be awarded for 15 days, which is the better prize? Explain your reasoning.

_____

_____

Learn!

When you look at a function from left to right, you can identify where the function is increasing, decreasing, and constant.

- If the *y*-values increase as the *x*-values increase, the function is **increasing**.
- If the *y*-values decrease as the *x*-values increase, the function is **decreasing**.
- If the *y*-values stay the same as the *x*-values increase, the function is **constant**.

Look at the example.

This graph shows the altitude of an airplane during a flight. The function is increasing during interval 1 as the plane takes off. Then it remains constant during interval 2 as the plane flies. Finally, it is decreasing during interval 3 as the plane lands.

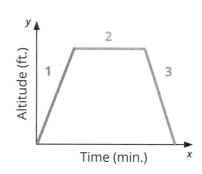

Determine whether each function is increasing, decreasing, or constant on each interval.

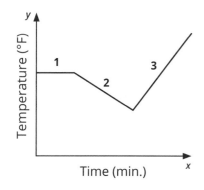

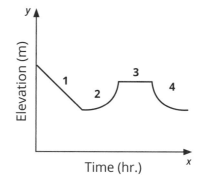

Interval 1: _____

Interval 2: _____

Interval 3: _____

Interval 1: _____

Interval 2: _____

Interval 3: _____

Interval 4: _____

Each story below can be modeled by a function. Match each story with its corresponding graph. Write the letter on the line.

_____ Paolo is on a train that is approaching the station. The train is slowing down gradually until it comes to a stop.

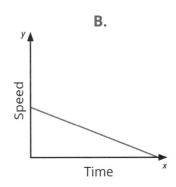

A.

B.

_____ Peyton is at the starting line of a race. She begins running, increasing her speed until she runs at a steady pace.

_____ Eva's family is driving on the highway. Their car is on cruise control going 55 miles per hour.

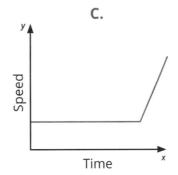

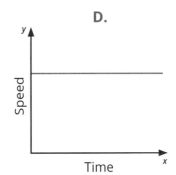

C.

D.

_____ Ryan is driving a go-kart. He pushes the gas pedal to speed up. Then he pushes the brake as he goes around a turn.

E.

F.

_____ Cameron is riding a bike down a hill.

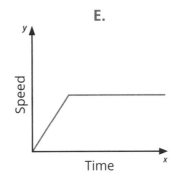

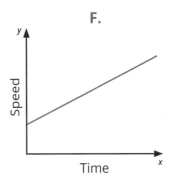

_____ A roller coaster car is being pulled up the first hill. Then it is released and goes down the hill.

Sketch a graph that could model each story.

In a 2-kilometer-long parade, the Eagles Marching Band marched 1 kilometer at a constant pace for 30 minutes. Then the band marched in place while they played a song for a big crowd. Finally, they continued marching until the end of the parade, which they reached after a total of 60 minutes.

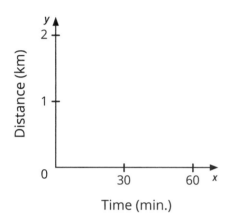

Roxy is test-driving a remote-controlled robot. The robot took 15 seconds to drive 10 meters away from the starting line at a constant speed. Then it immediately turned around and drove back to the start at a slower speed than before.

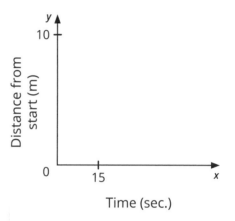

A bus driver waited at a bus stop for 5 minutes while he picked up some passengers. Then he drove the bus at a constant rate for 25 minutes before reaching Moonville Movie Theater, which was 20 miles away. He waited there for 5 minutes.

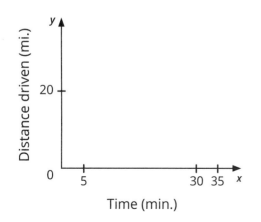

During a snowstorm, 4 inches of snow fell over a period of 3 hours. All the snow remained in place for 2 more hours. Then the temperature warmed up and started melting the snow at a steady rate. After 6 more hours, half of the snow had melted.

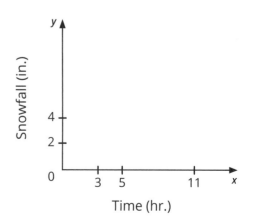

Use each story and its graph to answer the questions.

Vivian is running a race. She ran at a steady pace until she took a break to rest and drink water. Then she finished the race.

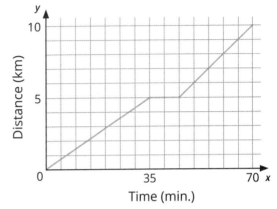

What was the total distance Vivian ran in the race?

_____

How long was Vivian's break?

_____

Did Vivian run faster before taking a break or after? Explain how you know.

_____

_____

Tyrone is hiking down a mountain trail. He descended at a constant rate until stopping to eat lunch. Then he had to hike up a small hill before hiking down the rest of the mountain.

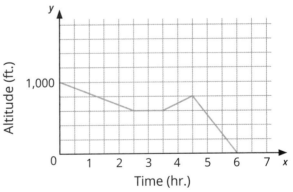

What was Tyrone's altitude during his lunch?

_____

How long did it take Tyrone to hike down the trail?

_____

At what rate did Tyrone descend the mountain during the first 2.5 hours?

_____

Challenge!

IXL.com
Checkpoint ID

K7A

Translations, **reflections**, and **rotations** are three types of transformations. These transformations map the original figure, or preimage, to a transformed figure, or image.

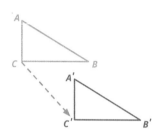

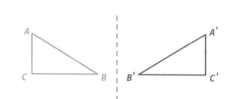

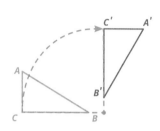

A **translation** moves a figure to a different location.

A **reflection** flips a figure over a line to create a mirror image.

A **rotation** turns a figure around a fixed point.

When a figure is translated, reflected, or rotated, the corresponding sides of the image and the preimage are equal in length, and the corresponding angles are equal in measure.

Each shape below has undergone a transformation to map the preimage to the image. Identify whether each transformation is a translation, reflection, or rotation.

preimage   image

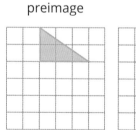 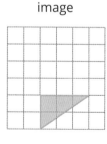

translation

(reflection)

rotation

preimage   image

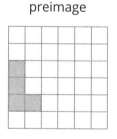 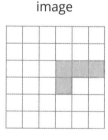

translation

reflection

rotation

preimage   image

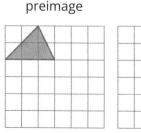 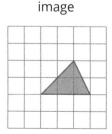

translation

reflection

rotation

Keep going! Identify whether each transformation is a translation, reflection, or rotation.

preimage	image	
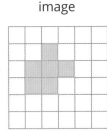		translation reflection rotation

preimage	image	
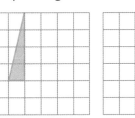		translation reflection rotation

preimage	image	
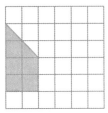		translation reflection rotation

preimage	image	
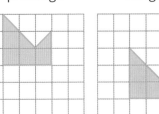		translation reflection rotation

preimage	image	
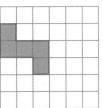		translation reflection rotation

preimage	image	
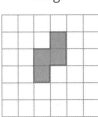		translation reflection rotation

preimage	image	
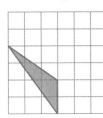		translation reflection rotation

preimage	image	
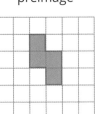		translation reflection rotation

Learn!

A **translation** is a transformation that moves a figure to a different location without changing its size or orientation. The preimage and image of a translated figure are congruent.

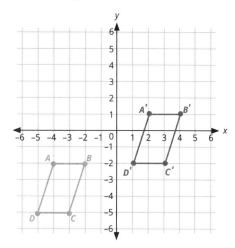

In this example, parallelogram *ABCD* was translated **6 units right** and **3 units up** to form parallelogram *A'B'C'D'*.

Each coordinate plane shows a preimage and its translated image. Write a sentence to describe how each figure was translated.

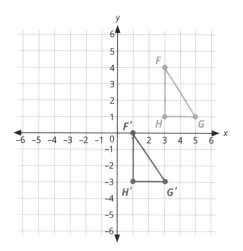

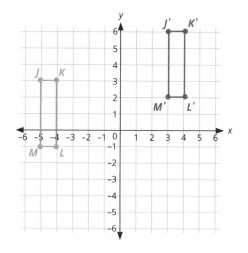

_____

_____

_____

_____

THINK ABOUT IT! In the translation of △*FGH* above, write the coordinates of vertex *F* and its image *F'*. How do the *x*- and *y*-coordinates change? Why do you think that is?

Learn!

You can use a rule to find the coordinates of a translated figure.

Any translation rule can be written as $(x, y) \mapsto (x + h, y + k)$. This means that if the point (x, y) lies on a figure, the point $(x + h, y + k)$ will lie on the translated figure.

- When translating right, h is positive. When translating left, h is negative.
- When translating up, k is positive. When translating down, k is negative.

Try using the rule to translate $\triangle ABC$ **3 units left** and **2 units up**. For this translation, $h = -3$ and $k = 2$, so $(x, y) \mapsto (x - 3, y + 2)$.

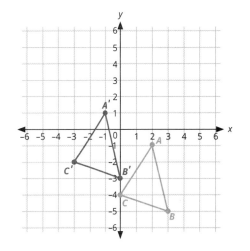

$A(2, -1) \mapsto A'(2 - 3, -1 + 2) = A'(-1, 1)$

$B(3, -5) \mapsto B'(3 - 3, -5 + 2) = B'(0, -3)$

$C(0, -4) \mapsto C'(0 - 3, -4 + 2) = C'(-3, -2)$

Find the coordinates of each translated figure.

$\triangle STU$ is translated 1 unit right and 4 units up. What are the coordinates of the resulting vertices?

$S(-5, 4)$ $T(-3, 2)$ $U(-5, 0)$

$S'(\underline{\quad}, \underline{\quad})$ $T'(\underline{\quad}, \underline{\quad})$ $U'(\underline{\quad}, \underline{\quad})$

Parallelogram $JKLM$ is translated 2 units left and 5 units down. What are the coordinates of the resulting vertices?

$J(-2, 4)$ $K(3, 4)$ $L(-3, 1)$ $M(2, 1)$

$J'(\underline{\quad}, \underline{\quad})$ $K'(\underline{\quad}, \underline{\quad})$ $L'(\underline{\quad}, \underline{\quad})$ $M'(\underline{\quad}, \underline{\quad})$

IXL.com
skill ID
RUP

Graph the image of each figure by completing the given translation.

Graph the image of ΔABC after a translation 4 units left and 2 units down.

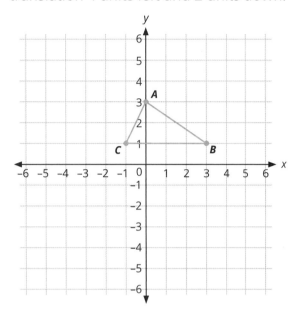

Graph the image of ΔTUV after a translation 1 unit right and 3 units up.

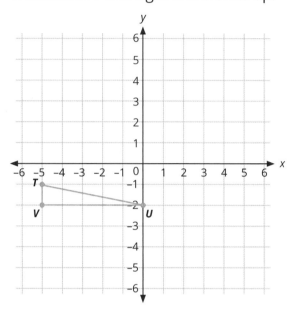

Graph the image of rectangle PQRS after a translation 3 units left and 6 units up.

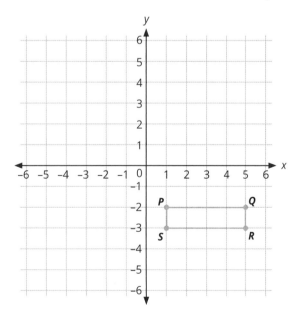

Graph the image of ΔJKL after a translation 3 units right and 2 units down.

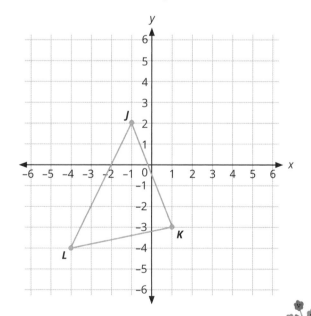

Keep going! Graph the image of each figure by completing the given translation.

Graph the image of rhombus *JKLM* after a translation 2 units left and 7 units up.

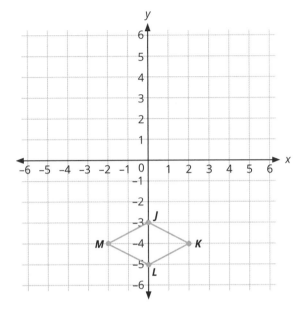

Graph the image of square *PQRS* after a translation 1 unit right and 5 units up.

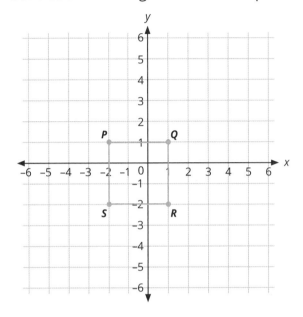

Graph the image of parallelogram *ABCD* after a translation 2 units right and 3 units down.

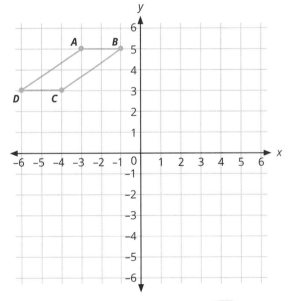

Learn!

A **reflection** is a transformation that flips a figure over a line to create a mirror image. The preimage and image of a reflected figure are congruent.

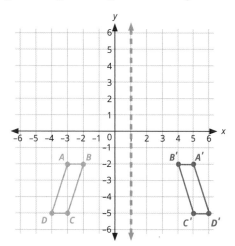

In this example, parallelogram *ABCD* was reflected across the line **x = 1** to form parallelogram *A'B'C'D'*.

Each coordinate plane shows a preimage and its reflected image. Write a sentence to describe how each figure was reflected.

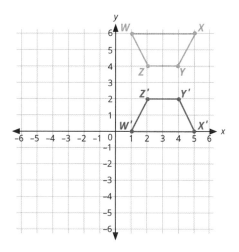

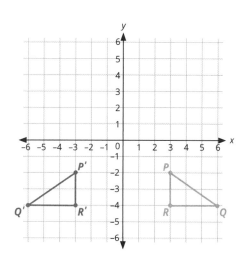

_____

_____

_____

_____

THINK ABOUT IT! In the reflection of △*PQR* above, write the coordinates of vertex *P* and its image *P'*. How do the *x*- and *y*-coordinates change? Why do you think that is?

Learn!

You can use these rules to find the coordinates of a reflected figure:

When a figure is reflected across the x-axis:	• x-coordinate stays the same • y-coordinate is the **opposite**	$(x, y) \mapsto (x, -y)$
When a figure is reflected across the y-axis:	• x-coordinate is the **opposite** • y-coordinate stays the same	$(x, y) \mapsto (-x, y)$
When a figure is reflected across any line:	Each point in the image is the same distance from the line of reflection as its corresponding point in the preimage.	

Try reflecting $\triangle ABC$ across the y-axis.
Use the rule $(x, y) \mapsto (-x, y)$.

$A(-2, 4) \quad \mapsto \quad A'(2, 4)$

$B(-2, -1) \quad \mapsto \quad B'(2, -1)$

$C(-5, 3) \quad \mapsto \quad C'(5, 3)$

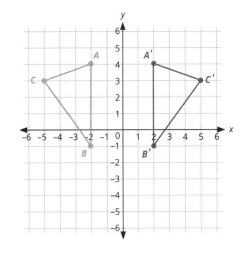

Find the coordinates of each reflected figure.

$\triangle QRS$ is reflected across the x-axis. What are the coordinates of the resulting vertices?

$Q(5, 4) \qquad R(4, 2) \qquad S(-1, 1)$

$Q'(\underline{\quad}, \underline{\quad}) \quad R'(\underline{\quad}, \underline{\quad}) \quad S'(\underline{\quad}, \underline{\quad})$

Parallelogram *DEFG* is reflected across the y-axis. What are the coordinates of the resulting vertices?

$D(3, 2) \qquad E(6, 3) \qquad F(6, 0) \qquad G(3, -1)$

$D'(\underline{\quad}, \underline{\quad}) \quad E'(\underline{\quad}, \underline{\quad}) \quad F'(\underline{\quad}, \underline{\quad}) \quad G'(\underline{\quad}, \underline{\quad})$

IXL.com
skill ID
5UM

Graph the image of each figure by completing the given reflection.

Graph the image of △*ABC* after a reflection across the *x*-axis.

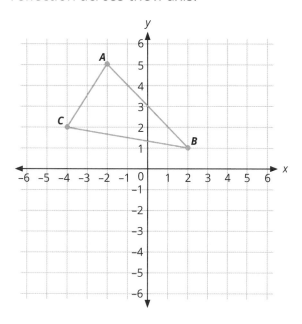

Graph the image of parallelogram *WXYZ* after a reflection across the *x*-axis.

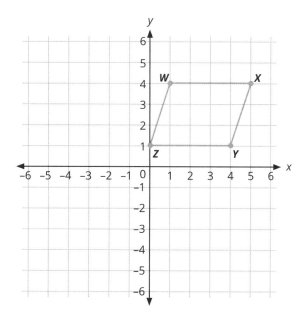

Graph the image of square *PQRS* after a reflection across the *y*-axis.

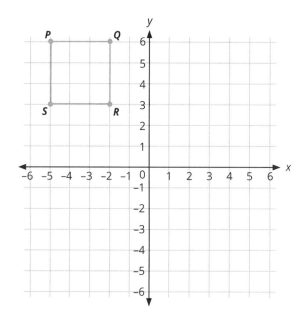

IXL.com
skill ID
74Z

Keep going! Graph the image of each figure by completing the given reflection.

Graph the image of trapezoid *JKLM* after a reflection across the line *y* = –2.

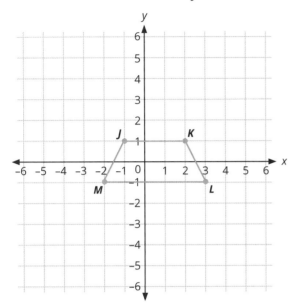

Graph the image of △*RST* after a reflection across the line *x* = –1.

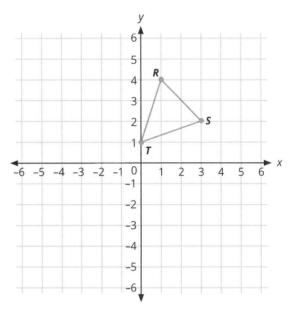

Graph the image of △*PQR* after a reflection across the line *y* = 3.

Learn!

A **rotation** is a transformation that turns a figure around a fixed point. The preimage and image of a rotated figure are congruent.

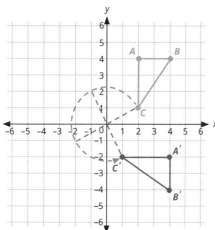

In this example, $\triangle ABC$ was rotated **270° counterclockwise** around the origin to form $\triangle A'B'C'$.

Each coordinate plane shows a figure that was rotated counterclockwise to produce its image. Write a sentence to describe how each figure was rotated.

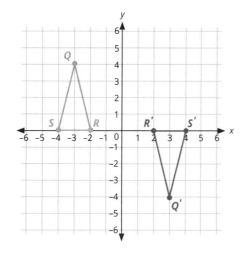

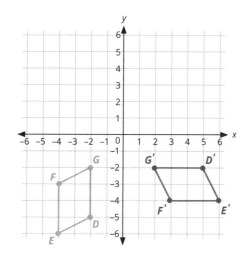

_____

_____

_____

_____

DIG DEEPER! In the rotation of $\triangle QRS$ above, write the coordinates of vertex Q and its image Q'. How do the x- and y-coordinates change? Why do you think that is?

You can use these rules to find the coordinates of a figure that has been rotated around the origin:

Angle of rotation	Rule
90° counterclockwise	$(x, y) \mapsto (-y, x)$
180° counterclockwise	$(x, y) \mapsto (-x, -y)$
270° counterclockwise	$(x, y) \mapsto (y, -x)$

Try rotating $\triangle ABC$ 90° counterclockwise around the origin. Use the rule $(x, y) \mapsto (-y, x)$.

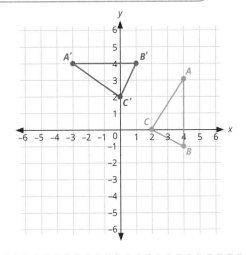

$A(4, 3) \mapsto A'(-3, 4)$

$B(4, -1) \mapsto B'(1, 4)$

$C(2, 0) \mapsto C'(0, 2)$

Find the coordinates of each rotated figure.

$\triangle VWX$ is rotated 270° counterclockwise around the origin. What are the coordinates of the resulting vertices?

$V(4, 0)$ $W(6, -5)$ $X(2, -4)$

$V'(\rule{1cm}{0.1pt} , \rule{1cm}{0.1pt})$ $W'(\rule{1cm}{0.1pt} , \rule{1cm}{0.1pt})$ $X'(\rule{1cm}{0.1pt} , \rule{1cm}{0.1pt})$

Quadrilateral $JKLM$ is rotated 180° counterclockwise around the origin. What are the coordinates of the resulting vertices?

$J(-3, -2)$ $K(-1, -2)$ $L(-1, -5)$ $M(-4, -5)$

$J'(\rule{1cm}{0.1pt} , \rule{1cm}{0.1pt})$ $K'(\rule{1cm}{0.1pt} , \rule{1cm}{0.1pt})$ $L'(\rule{1cm}{0.1pt} , \rule{1cm}{0.1pt})$ $M'(\rule{1cm}{0.1pt} , \rule{1cm}{0.1pt})$

IXL.com
skill ID

HHS

Graph the image of each figure by completing the given rotation.

Graph the image of △*ABC* after a rotation 180° counterclockwise around the origin.

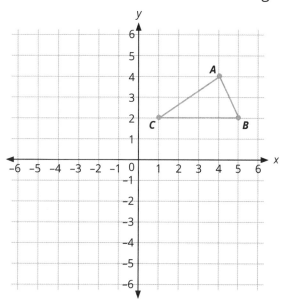

Graph the image of △*PQR* after a rotation 90° counterclockwise around the origin.

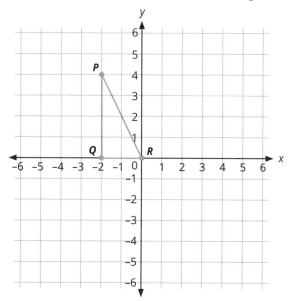

Graph the image of △*UVW* after a rotation 180° counterclockwise around the origin.

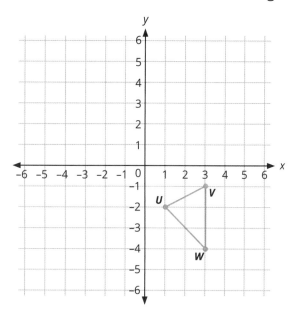

Graph the image of rectangle *DEFG* after a rotation 270° counterclockwise around the origin.

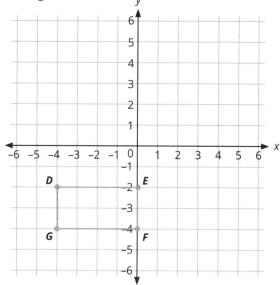

DIG DEEPER! Look at the last problem again. Try rotating rectangle *DEFG* 90° clockwise around the origin. You should end up with the same image!

Keep going! Graph the image of each figure by completing the given rotation.

Graph the image of trapezoid *KLMN* after a rotation 90° counterclockwise around the origin.

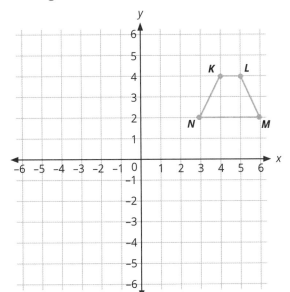

Graph the image of △*STU* after a rotation 270° counterclockwise around the origin.

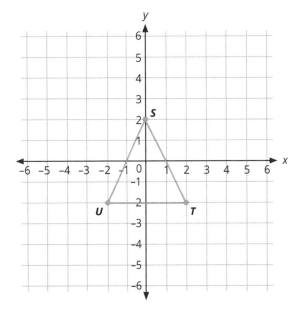

Graph the image of rhombus *EFGH* after a rotation 90° counterclockwise around the origin.

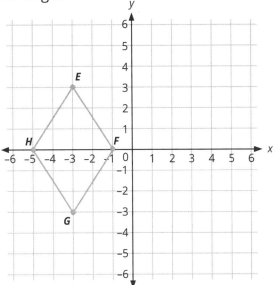

A figure can go through multiple transformations one after the other. This is called a **sequence of transformations**. Complete each sequence of transformations described below. You can draw each figure after the first transformation to help you along the way.

Graph the image of △ABC after a rotation 90° counterclockwise around the origin and a reflection over the x-axis.

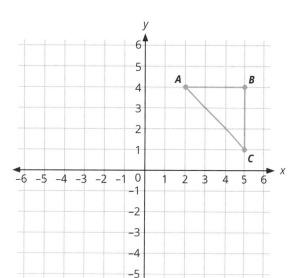

Graph the image of △STU after a translation 5 units right and 1 unit up and a reflection over the line x = 3.

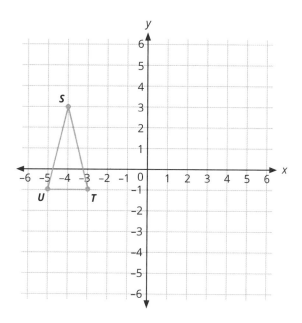

Graph the image of parallelogram TUVW after a translation 2 units left and 3 units up and a reflection over the line x = –1.

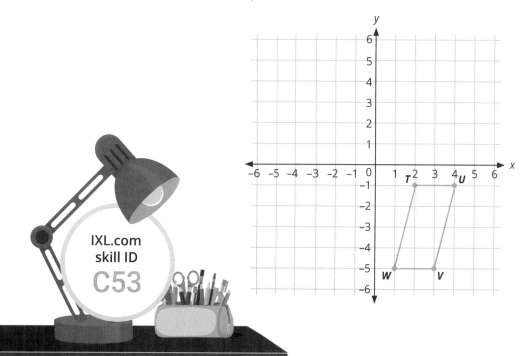

IXL.com
skill ID
C53

Keep going! Graph each sequence of transformations.

Graph the image of rectangle *GHJK* after a translation 4 units right and 1 unit down and a rotation 180° counterclockwise around the origin.

Graph the image of trapezoid *ABCD* after a rotation 180° counterclockwise around the origin and a reflection over the line $y = -2$.

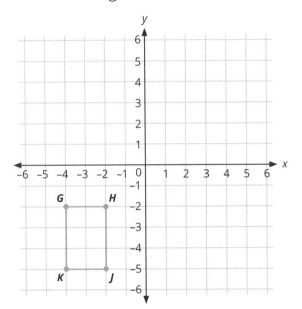

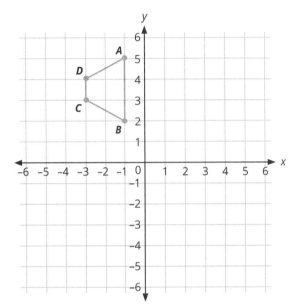

THINK ABOUT IT!   Look at the first problem again. How does the area of rectangle *GHJK* compare to the area of its image *G'H'J'K'*?

Congruent figures are the same size and shape. Their corresponding sides have equal lengths, and their corresponding angles have equal measures. If two figures are congruent, you can map one figure onto the other using a sequence of translations, reflections, and rotations.

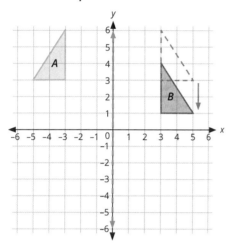

To see if figure A and figure B are congruent, try to find a sequence of transformations that maps one figure onto the other.

You can map figure A onto figure B by a **reflection across the y-axis** and a **translation 2 units down**.

So, figure A and figure B are congruent.

Determine whether the figures in each coordinate plane are congruent or not congruent. If the figures are congruent, describe a sequence of transformations that maps one figure onto the other. If they are not congruent, explain why.

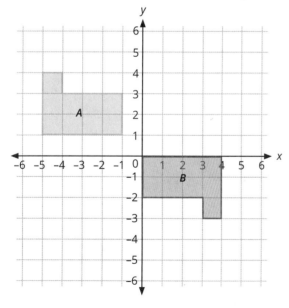

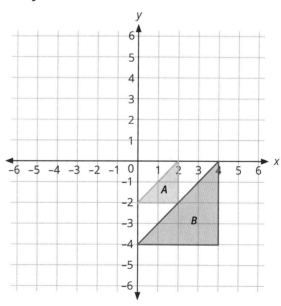

_____

_____

_____

_____

Keep going! Determine if the figures in each coordinate plane are congruent or not congruent. If the figures are congruent, describe a sequence of transformations that maps one figure onto the other. If they are not congruent, explain why.

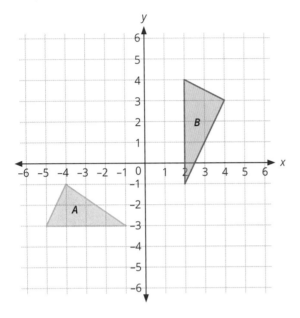

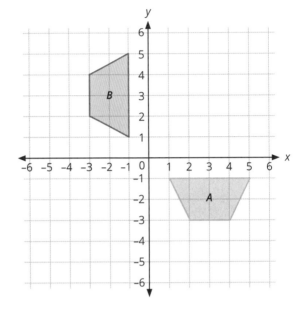

_____

_____

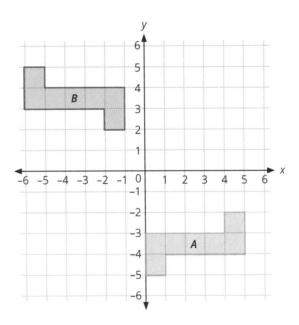

_____

_____

Exploration Zone

A **tessellation** is the covering of a flat surface with one or more repeating geometric shapes. The shapes must fit together with no overlaps and no gaps. Quilt patterns, tiled floors, and honeycomb are all examples of tessellations.

Transformations can be used to help create tessellations. Shapes can be translated, reflected, or rotated to cover a flat surface. Only a few regular polygons can tessellate. Look at the examples below.

Here is a tessellation with an equilateral triangle. The triangles fit together with no gaps or overlaps, so an equilateral triangle can tessellate.

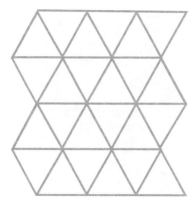

Here is what happens when you try to tessellate a regular pentagon. There are gaps when you try to fit the pentagons together, so a regular pentagon **cannot** tessellate.

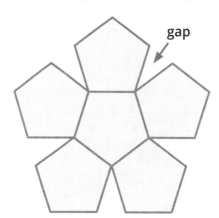

gap

Determine if each regular polygon below can tessellate. You can use a ruler, tracing paper, or another tool to help you.

As a next step, try creating your own tessellation that is made up of more than one shape!

Learn!

A **dilation** is a transformation that changes the size of a figure without changing its shape. Figures are dilated from a fixed point called the **center of dilation**. The **scale factor** tells you how much the dilation enlarges or reduces the figure. You can find the scale factor by finding the ratio of lengths in the image to the corresponding lengths in the preimage.

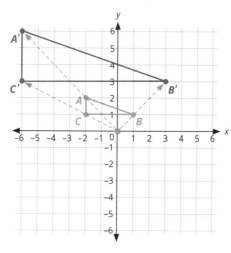

In this example, ΔABC was dilated from the origin to form ΔA'B'C'.

Sides $\overline{BC}$ and $\overline{B'C'}$ correspond. Divide the length of the image by the length of the preimage to find the scale factor. So, the scale factor is equal to $\frac{9}{3}$ = 3.

ΔABC was dilated from the origin by a scale factor of 3 to form ΔA'B'C'.

Each coordinate plane shows a figure and its image after a dilation centered at the origin. Write a sentence to describe how each figure was dilated.

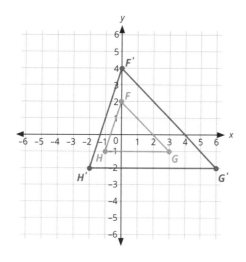

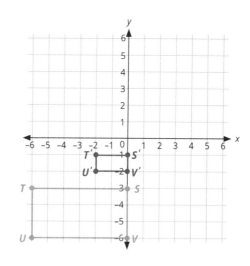

_____

_____

_____

_____

DIG DEEPER! In the dilation of ΔFGH above, write the coordinates of vertex G and its image G'. How do the x- and y-coordinates change? Why do you think that is?

Learn!

You can use a rule to find the coordinates of a figure that has been dilated by a scale factor of k, centered at the origin:

$$(x, y) \mapsto (kx, ky)$$

When $k > 1$, the image is larger than the preimage.

When $0 < k < 1$, the image is smaller than the preimage.

Try using the rule to dilate $\triangle ABC$ by a scale factor of $\frac{1}{2}$, centered at the origin.

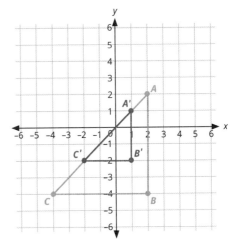

$A(2, 2) \quad \mapsto \quad A'\left(\frac{1}{2} \cdot 2, \frac{1}{2} \cdot 2\right) \quad = \quad A'(1, 1)$

$B(2, -4) \quad \mapsto \quad B'\left(\frac{1}{2} \cdot 2, \frac{1}{2} \cdot (-4)\right) \quad = \quad B'(1, -2)$

$C(-4, -4) \quad \mapsto \quad C'\left(\frac{1}{2} \cdot (-4), \frac{1}{2} \cdot (-4)\right) \quad = \quad C'(-2, -2)$

Find the coordinates of each dilated figure.

Parallelogram *DEFG* is dilated by a scale factor of 4, centered at the origin. What are the coordinates of the resulting vertices?

$D(0, 1) \qquad E(2, 1) \qquad F(1, -3) \qquad G(-1, -3)$

$D'(\underline{\quad}, \underline{\quad}) \quad E'(\underline{\quad}, \underline{\quad}) \quad F'(\underline{\quad}, \underline{\quad}) \quad G'(\underline{\quad}, \underline{\quad})$

$\triangle VWX$ is dilated by a scale factor of $\frac{1}{4}$, centered at the origin. What are the coordinates of the resulting vertices?

$V(-8, -4) \qquad W(0, -4) \qquad X(4, 8)$

$V'(\underline{\quad}, \underline{\quad}) \quad W'(\underline{\quad}, \underline{\quad}) \quad X'(\underline{\quad}, \underline{\quad})$

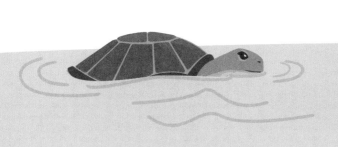

Graph the image of each figure by completing the given dilation.

Graph the image of △ABC after a dilation with a scale factor of 2, centered at the origin.

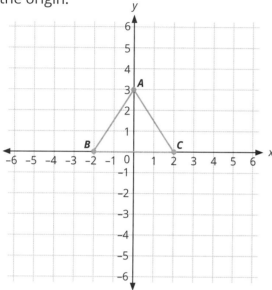

Graph the image of △LMN after a dilation with a scale factor of $\frac{1}{2}$, centered at the origin.

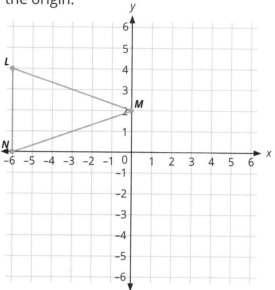

Graph the image of parallelogram QRST after a dilation with a scale factor of 4, centered at the origin.

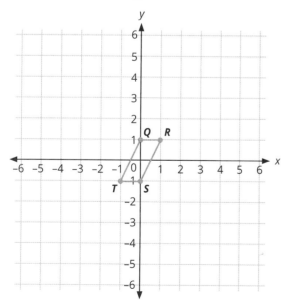

Graph the image of △UVW after a dilation with a scale factor of $\frac{1}{3}$, centered at the origin.

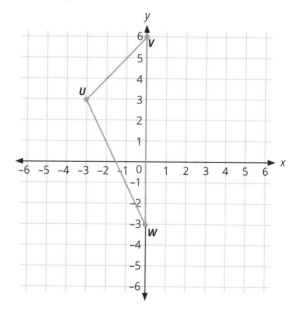

Keep going! Graph the image of each figure by completing the given dilation.

Graph the image of square *DEFG* after a dilation with a scale factor of $\frac{3}{4}$, centered at the origin.

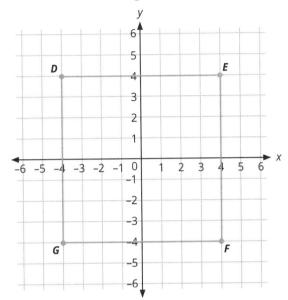

Graph the image of trapezoid *PQRS* after a dilation with a scale factor of 3, centered at the origin.

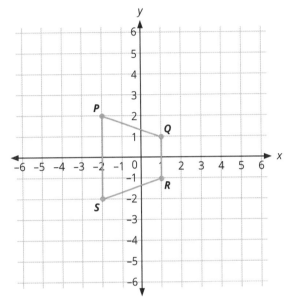

Graph the image of kite *KLMN* after a dilation with a scale factor of $\frac{2}{3}$, centered at the origin.

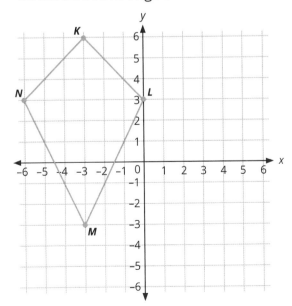

Learn!

Similar figures are the same shape but not necessarily the same size. Their corresponding angles have equal measures, and their corresponding sides are proportional. If two figures are similar, you can map one figure onto the other using a sequence of transformations.

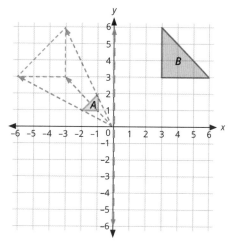

To see if figure *A* and figure *B* are similar, try to find a sequence of transformations that maps one figure onto the other.

You can map figure *A* onto figure *B* by a dilation with a scale factor of 3, centered at the origin, and then a reflection across the *y*-axis.

So, figure *A* and figure *B* are similar.

Determine if the figures in each coordinate plane are similar or not similar. If the figures are similar, describe a sequence of transformations that maps one figure onto the other. If they are not similar, explain why.

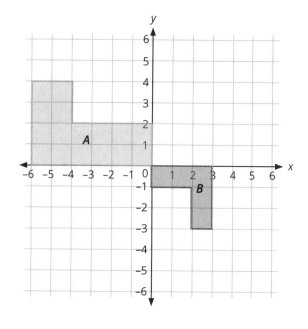

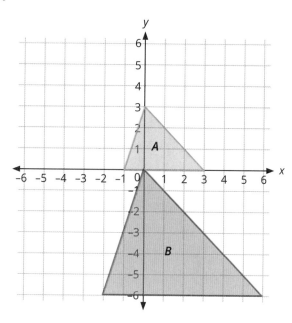

Keep going! Determine if the figures in each coordinate plane are similar or not similar. If the figures are similar, describe a sequence of transformations that maps one figure onto the other. If they are not similar, explain why.

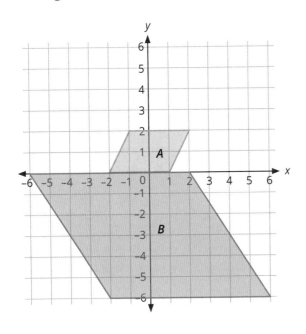

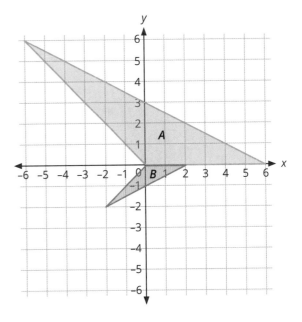

_____

_____

_____

_____

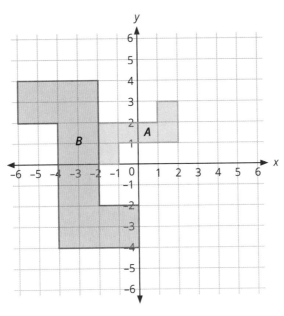

_____

_____

Exploration Zone

Similar triangles can help show that the slope of a line is constant. Take a look at the line and the three right triangles on the graph below.

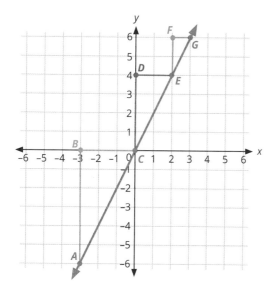

You can dilate △*EFG* by a scale factor of 2 and translate it to map it onto △*CDE*. So, △*EFG* is similar to △*CDE*.

You can also dilate △*EFG* by a scale factor of 3 and translate it to map it onto △*ABC*. So, △*EFG* is also similar to △*ABC*.

Since △*ABC* and △*CDE* are each similar to △*EFG*, △*ABC* and △*CDE* are also similar to each other.

How does this connect to the slope of the line? Fill in the table using the similar right triangles on the coordinate plane to find out.

Triangle	Length of vertical side	Length of horizontal side	Length of vertical side ÷ Length of horizontal side		
△*ABC*					
△*CDE*					
△*EFG*					

Because the three triangles are similar, the ratios of their vertical side length to their horizontal side length are the same. No matter which points you pick to find the slope of this line, you will draw another triangle that is similar to these. So, the slope of the line is always the same, or constant.

Use the relationship between slope and similar triangles to answer the questions below.

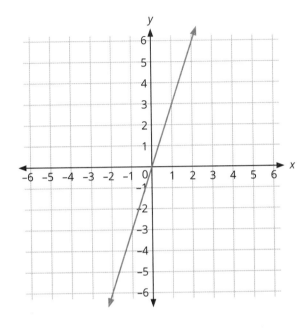

Find the slope of the line.

_____

If you drew a right triangle with a horizontal side length of 10 and its hypotenuse on this line, what would its vertical side length be?

_____

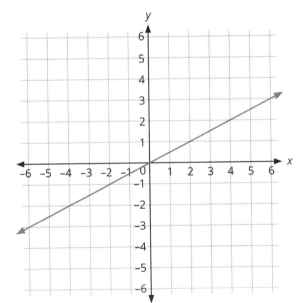

Find the slope of the line.

_____

If you drew a right triangle with a vertical side length of 12 and its hypotenuse on this line, what would its horizontal side length be?

_____

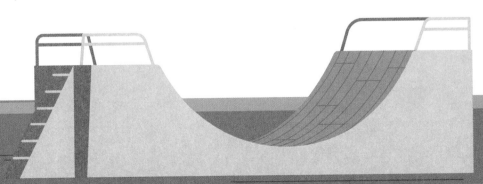

Use what you know about complementary, supplementary, vertical, and adjacent angles to find the value of each variable.

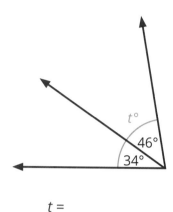

$t =$ _____

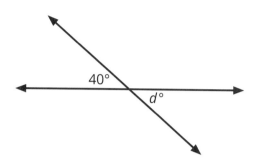

$d =$ _____

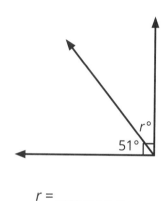

$r =$ _____

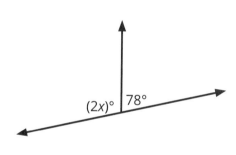

$x =$ _____

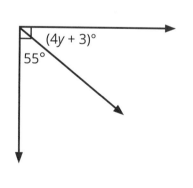

$y =$ _____

Learn!

A **transversal** is a line that intersects two or more other lines. When a transversal intersects two parallel lines, it creates eight angles. Some of the angle pairs have special names and relationships.

In the diagrams below, lines *a* and *b* are parallel, which is shown by the small triangle symbols on those lines. Line *t* is a transversal. Read about four different angle pair relationships:

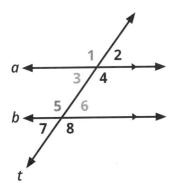

Corresponding angles are found in matching corners on the same side of the transversal. Since lines *a* and *b* are parallel, the corresponding angles are **congruent**. One pair of these angles here is ∠1 and ∠5. So, $m\angle 1 = m\angle 5$.

Alternate interior angles are found between the parallel lines on opposite sides of the transversal. Since lines *a* and *b* are parallel, the alternate interior angles are congruent. One pair of these angles here is ∠3 and ∠6. So, $m\angle 3 = m\angle 6$.

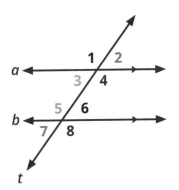

Alternate exterior angles are found outside the parallel lines on opposite sides of the transversal. Since lines *a* and *b* are parallel, the alternate exterior angles are congruent. One pair of these angles here is ∠2 and ∠7. So, $m\angle 2 = m\angle 7$.

Same-side interior angles are found between the parallel lines on the same side of the transversal. Since lines *a* and *b* are parallel, the same-side interior angles are supplementary. One pair of these angles here is ∠3 and ∠5. So, $m\angle 3 + m\angle 5 = 180°$.

Identify a pair of angles for each relationship.

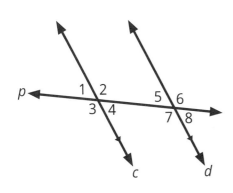

Corresponding angles: ∠2 and ∠6

Alternate interior angles: _____ and _____

Alternate exterior angles: _____ and _____

Same-side interior angles: _____ and _____

Congruent angles: _____ and _____

Find each missing angle measure. Then use angle relationships to help you explain.

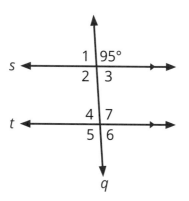

$m\angle 1 =$ _____ $m\angle 5 =$ _____

$m\angle 2 =$ _____ $m\angle 6 =$ _____

$m\angle 3 =$ _____ $m\angle 7 =$ _____

$m\angle 4 =$ _____

Explain how you found $m\angle 5$.

_____

_____

_____

Explain how you found $m\angle 7$.

_____

_____

_____

$m\angle 1 =$ _____ $m\angle 5 =$ _____

$m\angle 2 =$ _____ $m\angle 6 =$ _____

$m\angle 3 =$ _____ $m\angle 7 =$ _____

$m\angle 4 =$ _____

Explain how you found $m\angle 6$.

_____

_____

_____

CHALLENGE ZONE

Use what you know about transversals of parallel lines to find the value of each variable.

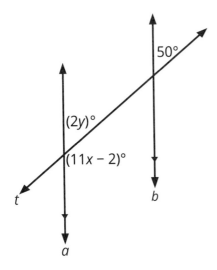

x = _____

y = _____

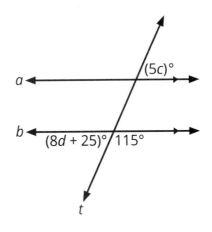

c = _____

d = _____

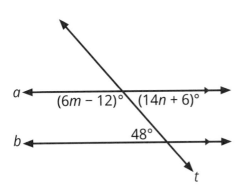

m = _____

n = _____

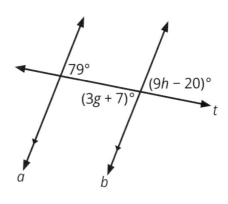

g = _____

h = _____

Learn!

The sum of the interior angle measures of a triangle is always 180°.

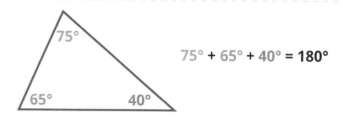

75° + 65° + 40° = **180°**

Find each missing angle measure.

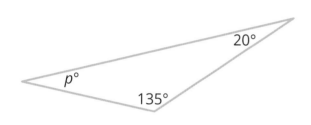

20°

p°

135°

p = _____

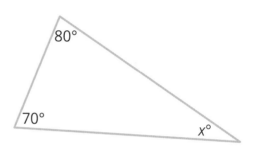

80°

70°

x°

x = _____

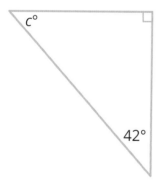

c°

42°

c = _____

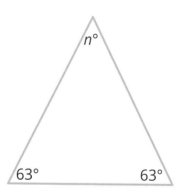

n°

63°   63°

n = _____

Keep going! Find each missing angle measure.

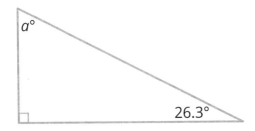

a = _____

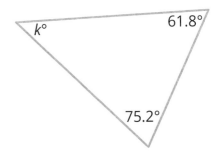

k = _____

v = _____

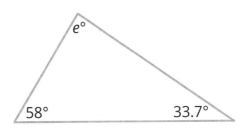

e = _____

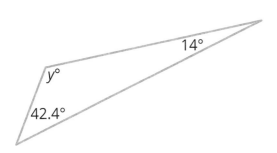

y = _____

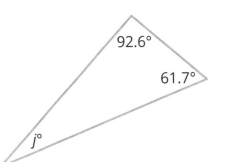

j = _____

Find the value of each variable.

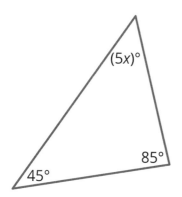

$x = $ _____

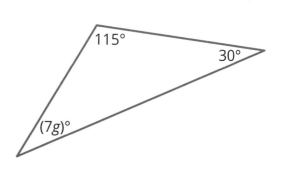

$g = $ _____

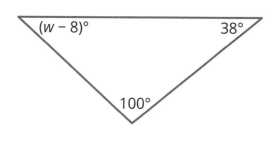

$w = $ _____

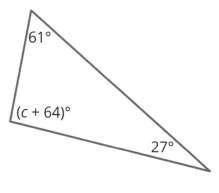

$c = $ _____

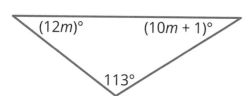

$m = $ _____

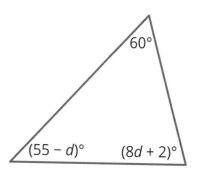

$d = $ _____

Use the diagram below to show that the sum of the interior angle measures of a triangle is 180°. Answer each question.

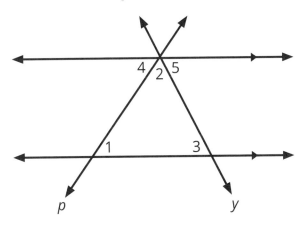

Name a pair of alternate interior angles created by the parallel lines and line *p*.

_____ and _____

Name a pair of alternate interior angles created by the parallel lines and line *y*.

_____ and _____

Since lines *p* and *y* intersect parallel lines, the pairs of alternate interior angles that you found above are congruent. Fill in the equations to show that the angle measures of the alternate interior angles are equal.

$m\angle 4 =$ _____ $m\angle 5 =$ _____

The diagram shows that $\angle 4$, $\angle 2$, and $\angle 5$ form a straight angle. Write an equation to show that the angle measures of those angles add up to 180°.

_____

Rewrite the equation that you just wrote. Substitute the angle measures that are equal to $m\angle 4$ and $m\angle 5$ into the equation.

_____

This equation shows that the interior angle measures of the triangle add up to 180°!

Learn!

An **exterior angle** of a triangle is created by extending one side of the triangle. The measure of an exterior angle of a triangle is equal to the sum of the two opposite interior angles.

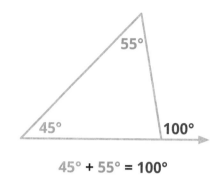

$$45° + 55° = 100°$$

Find each missing angle measure.

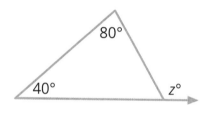

z = _____

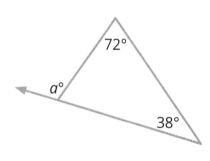

a = _____

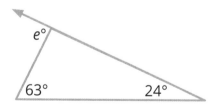

e = _____

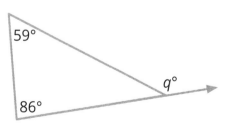

q = _____

Keep going! Find each missing angle measure.

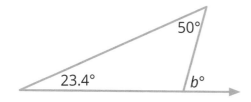

b = _____

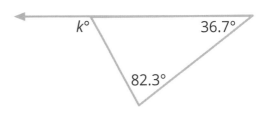

k = _____

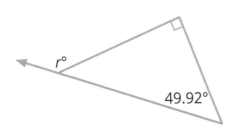

r = _____

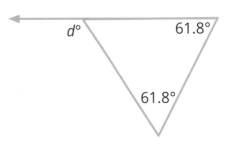

d = _____

y = _____

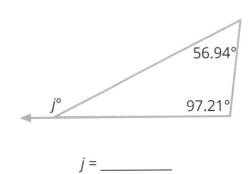

j = _____

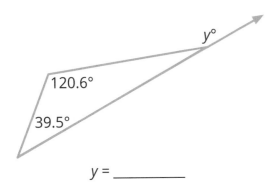

Find the value of each variable.

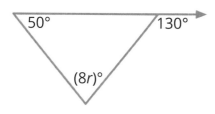

$r =$ _____

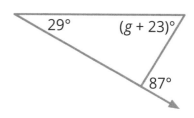

$g =$ _____

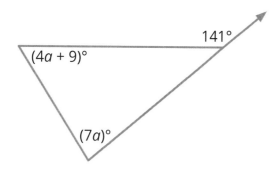

$a =$ _____

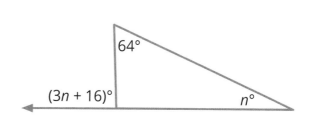

$n =$ _____

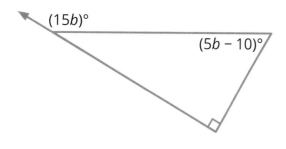

$b =$ _____

$y =$ _____

IXL.com skill ID

FMP

For more practice, visit IXL.com or the IXL mobile app and enter this code in the search bar.

Keep going! Find the value of each variable.

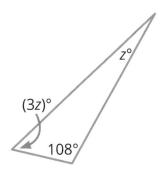

$z =$ _____

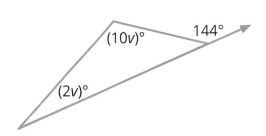

$v =$ _____

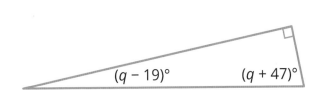

$q =$ _____

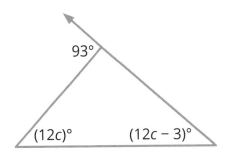

$c =$ _____

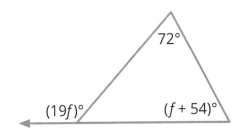

$f =$ _____

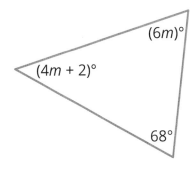

$m =$ _____

162 Interior and exterior angles of triangles

Answer each question.

A triangle has an interior angle that measures 22° and another interior angle that measures 61°. What is the measure of the third interior angle?

A right triangle has an acute interior angle that measures 57°. What is the measure of the triangle's other acute interior angle?

A triangle has interior angles that measure 48° and 36°. What is the measure of the exterior angle opposite those two angles?

A triangle has interior angles that measure $(6k + 7)°$, $(3k - 5)°$, and 61°. What is the value of k?

A triangle has an exterior angle that measures $(27r)°$. The interior angles opposite that exterior angle measure $(13r)°$ and $(16r - 8)°$. What is the value of r?

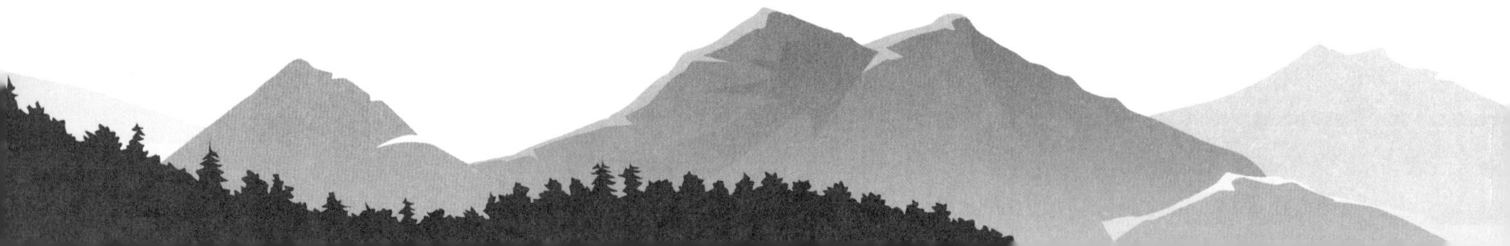

Find the value of each variable and the three angle measures of each triangle. Use what you know about transversals of parallel lines and interior and exterior angles of triangles to help.

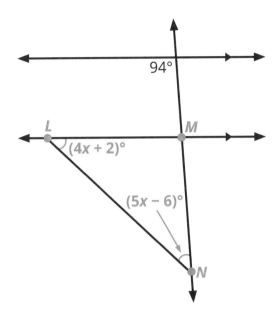

$x =$ _____

The measures of the angles of $\triangle LMN$ are

_____ , _____ , and _____ .

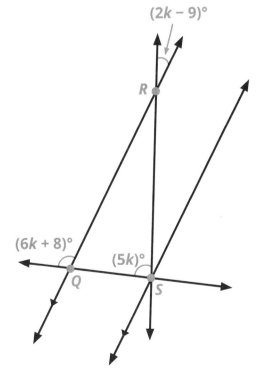

$k =$ _____

The measures of the angles of $\triangle QRS$ are

_____ , _____ , and _____ .

Challenge!

IXL.com
Checkpoint ID

EPV

Learn!

In a right triangle, the **hypotenuse** is the side that is opposite the right angle, and the **legs** are the two sides that form the right angle. The Pythagorean theorem describes a relationship among the sides of a right triangle. It states that the square of the hypotenuse is equal to the sum of the squares of the legs.

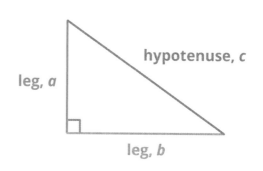

You can represent the Pythagorean theorem with the following equation, where *a* and *b* represent the lengths of the legs and *c* represents the length of the hypotenuse.

$$a^2 + b^2 = c^2$$

Use the Pythagorean theorem to find the length of each hypotenuse.

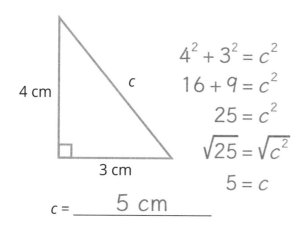

$$4^2 + 3^2 = c^2$$
$$16 + 9 = c^2$$
$$25 = c^2$$
$$\sqrt{25} = \sqrt{c^2}$$
$$5 = c$$

$c = $ _____5 cm_____

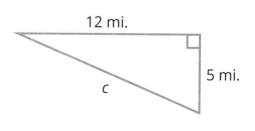

$c = $ _____

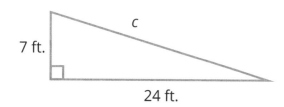

$c = $ _____

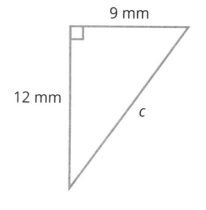

$c = $ _____

Keep going! Use the Pythagorean theorem to find the length of each hypotenuse. Round your answer to the nearest tenth, if necessary.

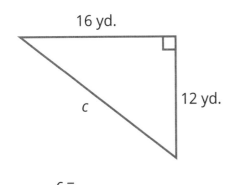

16 yd.

12 yd.

c

$c =$ _____

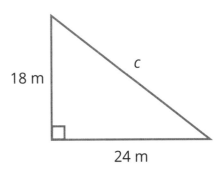

18 m

c

24 m

$c =$ _____

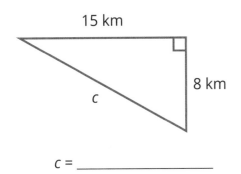

15 km

8 km

c

$c =$ _____

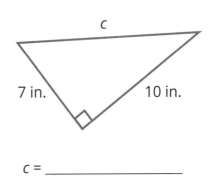

c

7 in.

10 in.

$c =$ _____

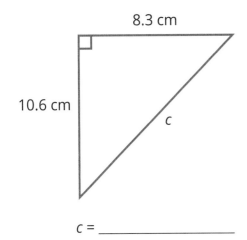

8.3 cm

10.6 cm

c

$c =$ _____

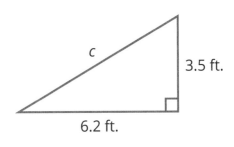

c

3.5 ft.

6.2 ft.

$c =$ _____

You can also use the Pythagorean theorem to find a missing leg length in a right triangle. Try it! Find each missing length.

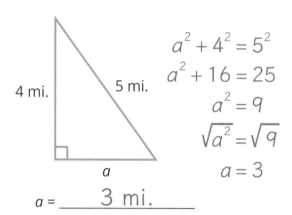

$$a^2 + 4^2 = 5^2$$
$$a^2 + 16 = 25$$
$$a^2 = 9$$
$$\sqrt{a^2} = \sqrt{9}$$
$$a = 3$$

$a =$ _____ 3 mi. _____

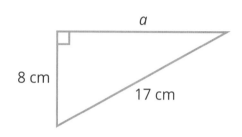

$a =$ _____

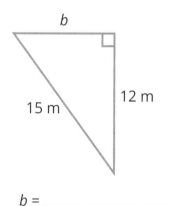

$b =$ _____

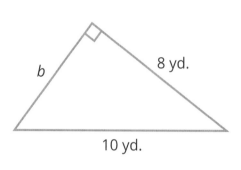

$b =$ _____

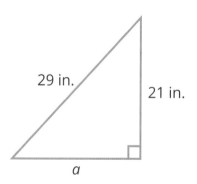

$a =$ _____

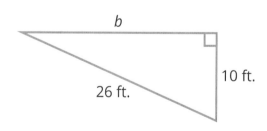

$b =$ _____

Keep going! Use the Pythagorean theorem to find each missing leg length. Round your answer to the nearest tenth, if necessary.

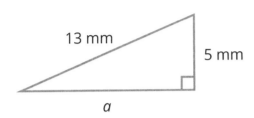

a = _____

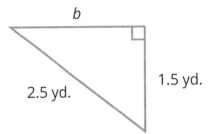

b = _____

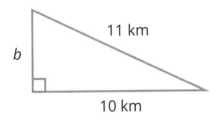

b = _____

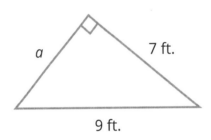

a = _____

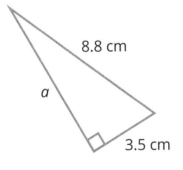

a = _____

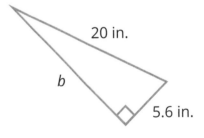

b = _____

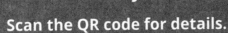

Use the Pythagorean theorem to find each missing side length. Round your answer to the nearest tenth, if necessary.

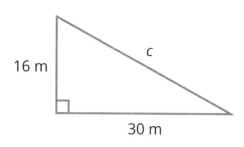

c = _____

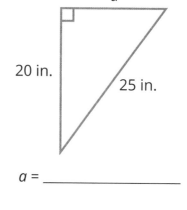

a = _____

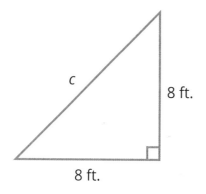

c = _____

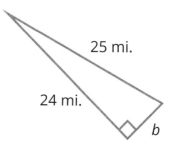

b = _____

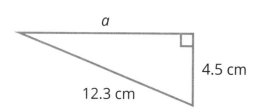

a = _____

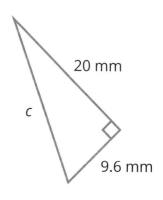

c = _____

Answer each question. Round your answer to the nearest tenth, if necessary.

Tom and Martin start a scavenger hunt at the same location in Lone Pine Forest. Tom travels 3 miles west. Martin travels 2.4 miles south. Measuring in a straight line, approximately how far apart are Tom and Martin?

_____

Kayla leans a 12-foot ladder against the wall she is painting. If the base of the ladder is 3 feet from the wall, approximately how far up the wall will the ladder reach?

_____

Ramon uses a square piece of paper with 7.5-centimeter side lengths for an origami project. He folds the paper into a right triangle by joining two opposite corners and creating a crease. What is the approximate length of the folded side?

_____

A television measures 60 inches along the diagonal line that passes through its center. The television is 29.4 inches tall. What is the approximate width of the television?

_____

Use what you know to prove the Pythagorean theorem.

Look at the large square below. Inside of the large square, there are four copies of a right triangle and a smaller square.

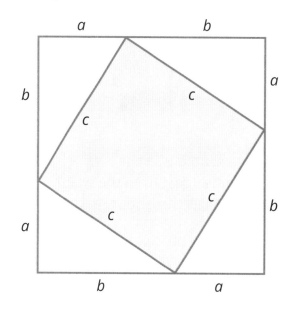

Write an expression to answer each question. Use an exponent when possible.

What is the area of the square with side lengths c? _____

What is the area of each triangle with side lengths a, b, and c? _____

Write the area of the large square by adding the areas of all the shapes inside it. Simplify your answer. _____

You can rearrange the four triangles from the previous page to fit inside the same large square together with two smaller squares. The large square still has side lengths $a + b$, so it has the same total area.

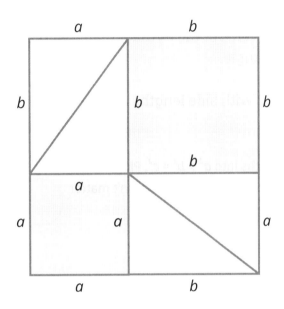

Write an expression to answer each question. Use an exponent when possible.

What is the area of the square with side lengths a? _____

What is the area of the square with side lengths b? _____

What is the area of each rectangle formed by two triangles? _____

Write the area of the large square by adding the areas of all the shapes inside it. Simplify your answer. _____

Since the large squares on both pages have the same area, write an equation that sets those areas equal to each other. Then get c^2 alone on one side of the equation.

Your equation shows that $a^2 + b^2 = c^2$. You proved the Pythagorean theorem!

Learn!

You can also use the converse of the Pythagorean theorem to determine if a triangle is acute, right, or obtuse. If a triangle has side lengths a, b, and c (where c is the longest side), you can follow these rules:

If $a^2 + b^2 > c^2$, then the triangle is **acute**.
If $a^2 + b^2 = c^2$, then the triangle is **right**.
If $a^2 + b^2 < c^2$, then the triangle is **obtuse**.

acute   right   obtuse

Determine whether each triangle is acute, right, or obtuse.

A triangle with side lengths of 5 kilometers, 3 kilometers, and 4 kilometers

| Acute | Right | Obtuse |

A triangle with side lengths of 14 feet, 16 feet, and 18 feet

| Acute | Right | Obtuse |

A triangle with side lengths of 9 yards, 12 yards, and 20 yards

| Acute | Right | Obtuse |

A triangle with side lengths of 22 miles, 17 miles, and 13 miles

| Acute | Right | Obtuse |

A triangle with side lengths of 15 centimeters, 20 centimeters, and 25 centimeters

| Acute | Right | Obtuse |

A triangle with side lengths of 9 meters, 12 meters, and 11 meters

| Acute | Right | Obtuse |

You can rearrange the four triangles from the previous page to fit inside the same large square together with two smaller squares. The large square still has side lengths $a + b$, so it has the same total area.

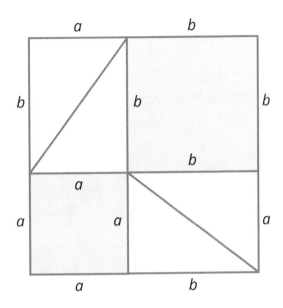

Write an expression to answer each question. Use an exponent when possible.

What is the area of the square with side lengths a? _____

What is the area of the square with side lengths b? _____

What is the area of each rectangle formed by two triangles? _____

Write the area of the large square by adding the areas of all the shapes inside it. Simplify your answer. _____

Since the large squares on both pages have the same area, write an equation that sets those areas equal to each other. Then get c^2 alone on one side of the equation.

Your equation shows that $a^2 + b^2 = c^2$. You proved the Pythagorean theorem!

Learn!

The converse of the Pythagorean theorem states that if a triangle has side lengths a, b, and c (where c is the longest side) and $a^2 + b^2 = c^2$, then the triangle is a right triangle. You can use the converse of the Pythagorean theorem to determine if three side lengths make a right triangle.

Try it! Determine if a triangle with side lengths of 10 feet, 12 feet, and 15 feet is a right triangle.

First, plug the given side lengths into $a^2 + b^2 = c^2$. Plug in the longest side for c. For the two shorter sides, it doesn't matter which is a and which is b.

Then, simplify.

$$a^2 + b^2 = c^2$$
$$10^2 + 12^2 \overset{?}{=} 15^2$$
$$100 + 144 \overset{?}{=} 225$$
$$244 \neq 225$$

Since 244 ≠ 225, a triangle with side lengths of 10 feet, 12 feet, and 15 feet is **not** a right triangle.

Determine if each set of side lengths makes a right triangle.

A triangle with side lengths of 7 centimeters, 24 centimeters, and 25 centimeters

Yes   No

A triangle with side lengths of 4 yards, 5 yards, and 6 yards

Yes   No

A triangle with side lengths of 12 miles, 24 miles, and 28 miles

Yes   No

A triangle with side lengths of 7 inches, 9 inches, and 11 inches

Yes   No

A triangle with side lengths of 8 kilometers, 15 kilometers, and 17 kilometers

Yes   No

IXL.com
skill ID
EQZ

Keep going! Determine if each set of side lengths makes a right triangle.

A triangle with side lengths of 12 millimeters, 9 millimeters, and 15 millimeters

A triangle with side lengths of 10 feet, 8 feet, and 6 feet

A triangle with side lengths of 6 kilometers, 14 kilometers, and 15 kilometers

A triangle with side lengths of 18 inches, 10 inches, and 12 inches

A triangle with side lengths of 7 yards, 15 yards, and 14 yards

A triangle with side lengths of 12 meters, 13 meters, and 5 meters

A triangle with side lengths of 16 meters, 20 meters, and 12 meters

A triangle with side lengths of 9 miles, 26 miles, and 25 miles

Learn!

You can also use the converse of the Pythagorean theorem to determine if a triangle is acute, right, or obtuse. If a triangle has side lengths a, b, and c (where c is the longest side), you can follow these rules:

If $a^2 + b^2 > c^2$, then the triangle is **acute**.
If $a^2 + b^2 = c^2$, then the triangle is **right**.
If $a^2 + b^2 < c^2$, then the triangle is **obtuse**.

acute right obtuse

Determine whether each triangle is acute, right, or obtuse.

A triangle with side lengths of 5 kilometers, 3 kilometers, and 4 kilometers

| Acute | Right | Obtuse |

A triangle with side lengths of 14 feet, 16 feet, and 18 feet

| Acute | Right | Obtuse |

A triangle with side lengths of 9 yards, 12 yards, and 20 yards

| Acute | Right | Obtuse |

A triangle with side lengths of 22 miles, 17 miles, and 13 miles

| Acute | Right | Obtuse |

A triangle with side lengths of 15 centimeters, 20 centimeters, and 25 centimeters

| Acute | Right | Obtuse |

A triangle with side lengths of 9 meters, 12 meters, and 11 meters

| Acute | Right | Obtuse |

Learn!

You can use the Pythagorean theorem to find the distance between two points on the coordinate plane. Try it! Find the distance between points Q and R.

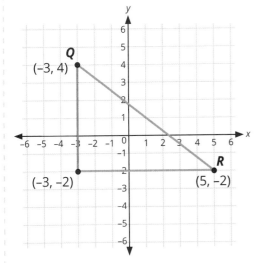

First, draw a right triangle that has a **hypotenuse** connecting points Q and R. Then, find the lengths of the legs.

To find the length of the **vertical leg**, find the absolute value of the difference of the y-coordinates of that leg's endpoints:
$$|4 - (-2)| = |6| = 6$$

To find the length of the **horizontal leg**, find the absolute value of the difference of the x-coordinates of that leg's endpoints:
$$|-3 - 5| = |-8| = 8$$

You can check the lengths you got above by counting the horizontal and vertical distances on the coordinate plane.

$$a^2 + b^2 = c^2$$
$$6^2 + 8^2 = c^2$$
$$36 + 64 = c^2$$
$$100 = c^2$$
$$\sqrt{100} = \sqrt{c^2}$$
$$10 = c$$

Finally, use the Pythagorean theorem to solve for the length of the hypotenuse, which is the distance between points Q and R.

So, the distance between points Q and R is 10 units.

Use the Pythagorean theorem to find the distance between each pair of points.

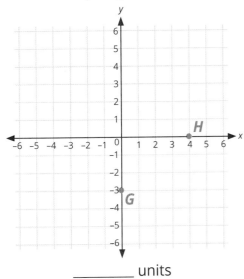

_____ units

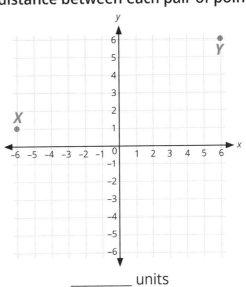

_____ units

Keep going! Find the distance between each pair of points. Round your answers to the nearest tenth.

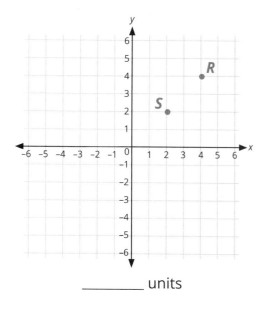

_____ units

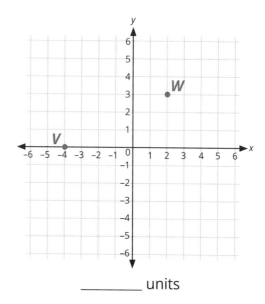

_____ units

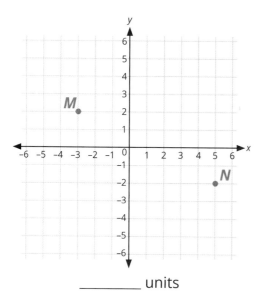

_____ units

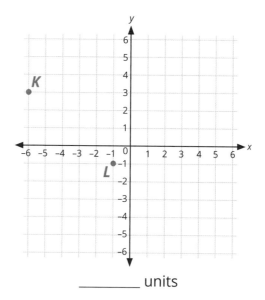

_____ units

Find the distance between the points. Plot the points to help you. Round your answers to the nearest tenth.

(0, 1) and (5, 3)

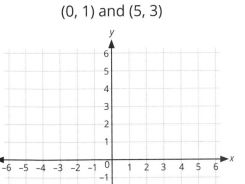

_____ units

(4, 3) and (1, –3)

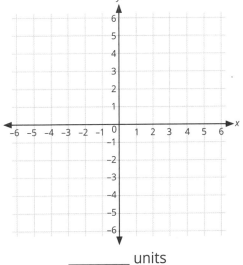

_____ units

(–5, 5) and (4, –4)

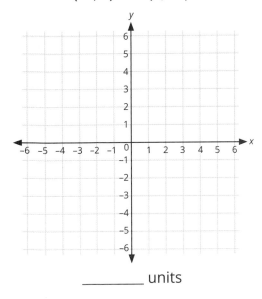

_____ units

(5, –3) and (–6, 5)

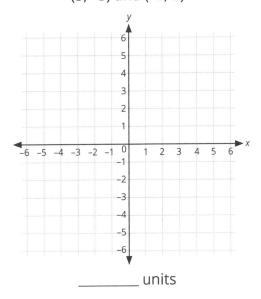

_____ units

Learn!

You can find the volume of a cylinder using its radius and height. Use the formula $V = \pi r^2 h$, where r is the **radius** and h is the **height**.

Try it! Find the volume of the cylinder. You can use 3.14 as an approximation for π.

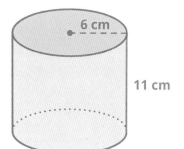

$V = \pi \cdot 6^2 \cdot 11$ Plug in the values of the radius and height.

$V \approx 1{,}243.44 \text{ cm}^3$ Simplify and include units.

Calculate the volume of each cylinder. If necessary, round your answer to the nearest hundredth.

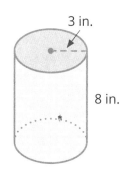

3 in.

8 in.

$V \approx$ _____

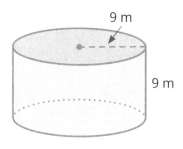

9 m

9 m

$V \approx$ _____

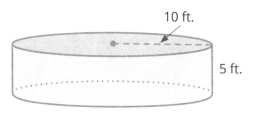

10 ft.

5 ft.

$V \approx$ _____

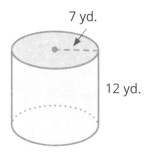

7 yd.

12 yd.

$V \approx$ _____

Keep going! Calculate the volume of each cylinder. If necessary, round your answer to the nearest hundredth. Remember that the diameter of a circle is twice its radius.

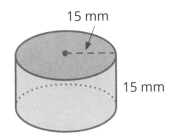

15 mm

15 mm

$V \approx$ _____

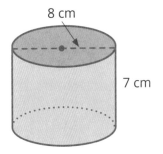

8 cm

7 cm

$V \approx$ _____

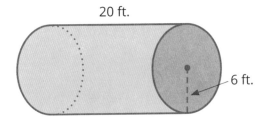

20 ft.

6 ft.

$V \approx$ _____

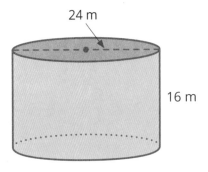

24 m

16 m

$V \approx$ _____

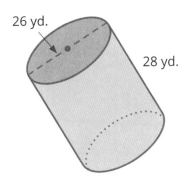

26 yd.

28 yd.

$V \approx$ _____

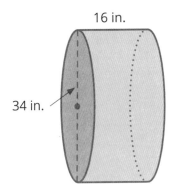

16 in.

34 in.

$V \approx$ _____

Learn!

You can find the volume of a cone using its radius and height. Use the formula $V = \frac{1}{3}\pi r^2 h$, where r is the **radius** and h is the **height**.

Try it! Find the volume of the cone. You can use 3.14 as an approximation for π.

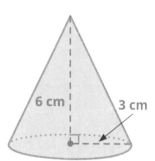

$V = \frac{1}{3}\pi \cdot 3^2 \cdot 6$ Plug in the values of the radius and height.

$V \approx 56.52 \text{ cm}^3$ Simplify and include units.

6 cm   3 cm

Calculate the volume of each cone. If necessary, round your answer to the nearest hundredth.

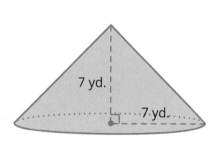

7 yd.

7 yd.

$V \approx$ _____

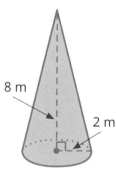

8 m

2 m

$V \approx$ _____

11 in.

5 in.

$V \approx$ _____

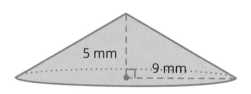

5 mm

9 mm

$V \approx$ _____

Keep going! Calculate the volume of each cone. If necessary, round your answer to the nearest hundredth.

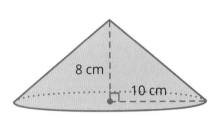

8 cm

10 cm

$V \approx$ _____

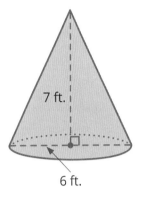

7 ft.

6 ft.

$V \approx$ _____

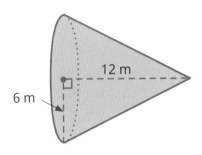

12 m

6 m

$V \approx$ _____

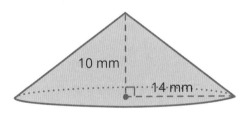

10 mm

14 mm

$V \approx$ _____

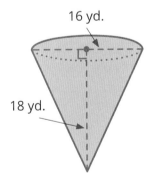

16 yd.

18 yd.

$V \approx$ _____

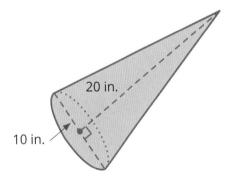

20 in.

10 in.

$V \approx$ _____

Learn!

You can find the volume of a sphere using its radius. Use the formula $V = \frac{4}{3}\pi r^3$, where r is the **radius**.

Try it! Find the volume of the sphere. You can use 3.14 as an approximation for π.

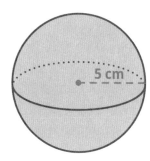

5 cm

$V = \frac{4}{3}\pi \cdot 5^3$ Plug in the value of the radius.

$V \approx 523.33 \text{ cm}^3$ Simplify and include units.

Calculate the volume of each sphere. If necessary, round your answer to the nearest hundredth.

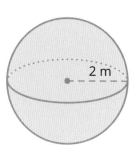

2 m

$V \approx$ _____

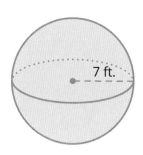

7 ft.

$V \approx$ _____

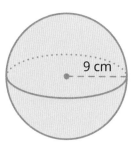

9 cm

$V \approx$ _____

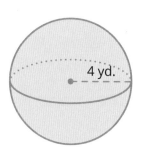

4 yd.

$V \approx$ _____

Keep going! Calculate the volume of each sphere. If necessary, round your answer to the nearest hundredth.

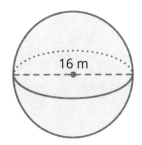

16 m

$V \approx$ _____

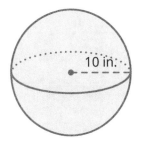

10 in.

$V \approx$ _____

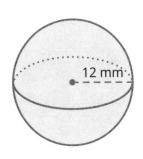

12 mm

$V \approx$ _____

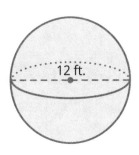

12 ft.

$V \approx$ _____

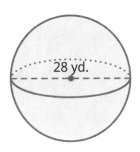

28 yd.

$V \approx$ _____

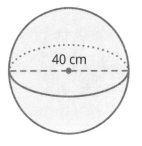

40 cm

$V \approx$ _____

CHALLENGE ZONE

Solve for each missing dimension. Use 3.14 for π.

The volume of a cylinder is approximately 452.16 cubic feet. The height of the cylinder is 9 feet. What is the cylinder's radius?

_____

The volume of a cone is approximately 376.8 millimeters. The radius of the cone is 6 millimeters. What is the cone's height?

_____

The volume of a cylinder is approximately 549.5 cubic inches. The radius of the cylinder is 5 inches. What is the cylinder's height?

_____

The volume of a sphere is approximately 113.04 cubic centimeters. What is the sphere's radius?

_____

Answer each question. If necessary, round your answer to the nearest hundredth.

Imani's family uses a cylindrical tank to collect rainwater. The tank has a radius of 2 feet and a height of 6 feet. What is the approximate volume of the tank?

_____

Tammy's Sweets and Treats serves snow cones in paper cones. Each paper cone has a radius of 4 centimeters and a height of 10 centimeters. What is the approximate volume of each paper cone?

_____

Mr. Quinn is a glassblower. He created a spherical piece of glass with a radius of 3 inches. What is the approximate volume of the piece of glass?

_____

Mila's kickball team got new kickballs. Each ball has a diameter of 10 inches. What is the approximate volume of one of the new kickballs?

_____

Learn!

A **scatter plot** is a type of graph that uses points to show values for two different variables. A scatter plot can show if there is a relationship, or **association**, between two variables.

Look at the examples of scatter plots below.

Positive association	Negative association	No association
	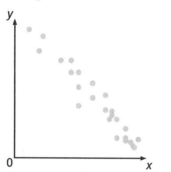	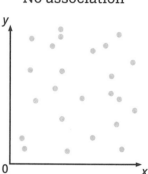
As *x*-values increase, *y*-values tend to increase.	As *x*-values increase, *y*-values tend to decrease.	There is no pattern between *x*-values and *y*-values.

Now, look at some other patterns you may see on a scatter plot.

An **outlier** is an extreme point that is set apart from the rest of the points.

A **cluster** is a group of points that are close together.

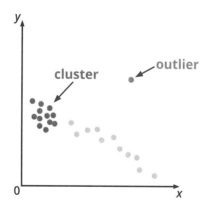

Determine whether each scatter plot shows a positive association, a negative association, or no association. Write your answer on the line. Then circle any outliers and draw a box around any clusters.

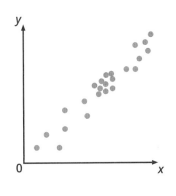

_____

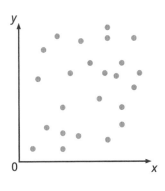

_____

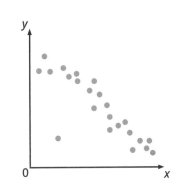

_____

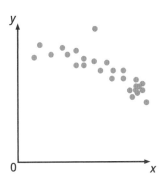

_____

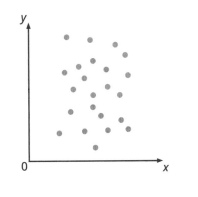

_____

Create a scatter plot for each data set.

Lila works at the concession stand at Quincy Stadium. Each day she works, she records the number of hot dogs and drinks she sells. She put the data into the table.

Hot dogs sold	10	8	16	9	18	6
Drinks sold	12	9	14	14	15	10

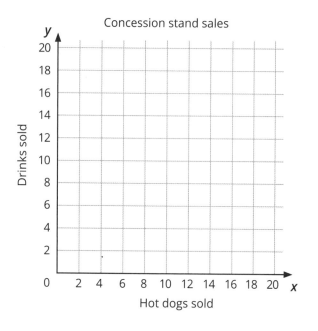

The table shows the numbers of pages and the prices for the most popular children's books at The Book Cellar.

Pages	8	16	24	16	12	28
Price ($)	12	18	15	9	22	25

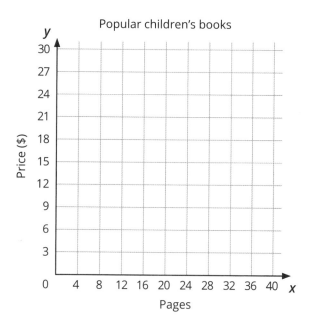

Create a scatter plot for each data set. Be sure to include a title, axis labels, and an appropriate scale for each scatter plot.

The table shows the average life span and weight for different breeds of dogs.

Weight (pounds)	5	60	30	20	75	95
Life span (years)	16	12	12	13	11	8

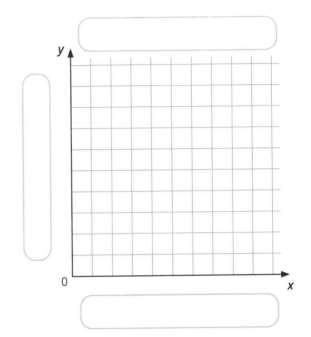

Each month for the last six months, Ms. Zhao recorded the average temperature and cost of her heating bill. She put the data into the table.

Average temperature (°C)	12	10	4	2	0	1
Heating bill total ($)	45	65	110	130	160	145

Challenge!

IXL.com
Checkpoint ID

DDR

Learn!

If a scatter plot shows a linear association, then a **line of best fit** can be used to represent the data. You can estimate a line of best fit by drawing a straight line that goes through as many points as possible, leaving about the same number of points above and below the line. The closer the data points are to the line of best fit, the stronger the association. Below are two scatter plots with lines of best fit that show different types of associations.

Strong positive association

Weak negative association

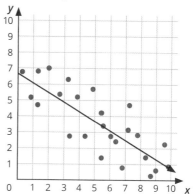

Estimate the line of best fit by sketching it on each scatter plot. Then write the type of association the scatter plot shows.

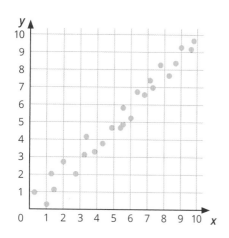

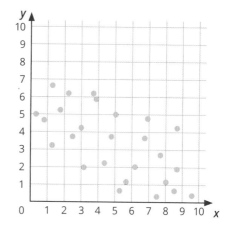

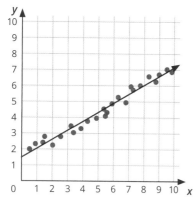

Keep going! Estimate the line of best fit by sketching it on each scatter plot. Then write the type of association the scatter plot shows.

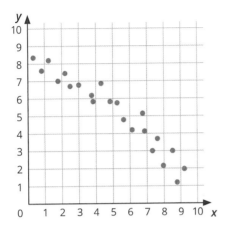

_____

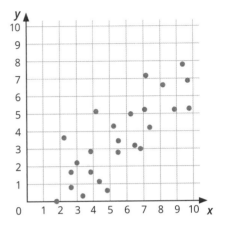

_____

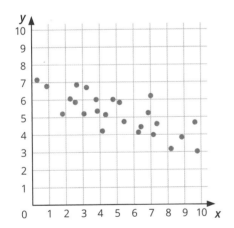

_____

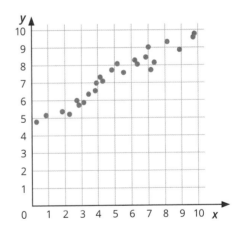

_____

Read each story. Then use the scatter plot and line of best fit to answer the questions.

Luca usually drinks at least one can of sparkling water a day. This scatter plot shows the relationship between the number of days since Luca's dad went grocery shopping and the number of cans of sparkling water left.

Write the equation of the line of best fit in slope-intercept form.

Slope = _____   y-intercept = _____

What does the slope mean in terms of the story?

_____

_____

What does the y-intercept mean in terms of the story?

_____

_____

Mr. Bryant owns the Double Scoop Ice Cream Truck. The scatter plot shows the relationship between the number of sunny days in a week and the number of ice cream cones Mr. Bryant sold.

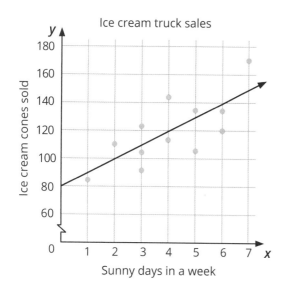

Write the equation of the line of best fit in slope-intercept form.

Slope = _____   y-intercept = _____

What does the slope mean in terms of the story?

_____

_____

What does the y-intercept mean in terms of the story?

_____

_____

Read each story. Then use the scatter plot and line of best fit to answer the questions.

The Lakemore Zoo has a special exhibit of baby bearded dragons. The scatter plot shows the relationship between the age and length of the bearded dragons.

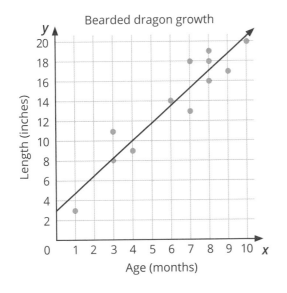

Bearded dragon growth

Write the equation of the line of best fit in slope-intercept form.

What length would you expect an 8-month-old bearded dragon to be?

_____

What age would you expect a 24-inch-long bearded dragon to be?

_____

At the beginning of the season, Coach Ty gives every member of the cross country team a 32-ounce reusable water bottle to use at each practice. The scatter plot shows the relationship between the kilometers each teammate ran and the water remaining in each runner's reusable water bottle at the end of a recent practice.

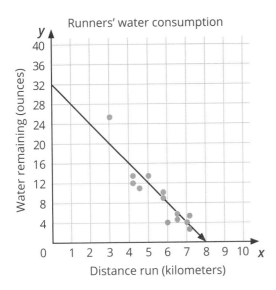

Runners' water consumption

Write the equation of the line of best fit in slope-intercept form.

How much water would you expect to be left in a runner's water bottle after a 5-kilometer run?

_____

If a runner drank 28 ounces from a full water bottle, how far would you expect the runner to have run during practice?

_____

Challenge!

IXL.com
Checkpoint ID

DEH

Learn!

Two-way frequency tables show frequencies for two categorical, or qualitative, variables. **Frequency** is the number of times a particular event occurs.

For example, this two-way frequency table shows observations about milkshakes sold at Snowy Peak Ice Cream Shop yesterday. The variables are flavor and size.

Joint frequencies tell about a combination of two categories. Each joint frequency in the table represents a flavor and size. For example, there were **34** small vanilla milkshakes sold.

Marginal frequencies are the totals for each category. There are four marginal frequencies in the table. For example, there were a total of **52** vanilla milkshakes sold.

	Small	Large	Total
Vanilla	34	18	52
Chocolate	27	24	51
Total	61	42	**103**

The bottom right corner shows the number of observations. So, there were **103** milkshakes sold in all.

Complete the two-way frequency table given the description.

There were 198 tickets sold for Rockridge Middle School's spring concert.

Of the tickets sold for Friday, 38 were student tickets and 55 were adult tickets.

Of the tickets sold for Saturday, 32 were student tickets and 73 were adult tickets.

	Student	Adult	Total
Friday			
Saturday			
Total			

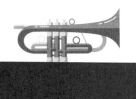

Keep going! Complete each two-way frequency table given the description.

The eighth graders at Holden Middle School went on a field trip to an art museum. Each student chose a main dish and a drink from the museum restaurant.

Of the students who chose a salad, 36 chose water and 28 chose juice.

Of the students who chose a sandwich, 22 chose water and 43 chose juice.

	Water	Juice	Total
Salad			
Sandwich			
Total			

Presto Pasta catered an event on Saturday and served 77 guests. They offered two pasta options and two sauces.

Of the orders for penne pasta, 14 had marinara and 6 had pesto.

Of the orders for angel hair, 31 had marinara.

	Marinara	Pesto	Total
Penne			
Angel hair			
Total			

The Grand County Fair had 164 visitors today.

There were 121 total visitors who bought food and 87 total visitors who played arcade games.

There were 28 visitors who didn't buy food or play arcade games.

	Food	No food	Total
Arcade			
No arcade			
Total			

Answer each question using the data in the two-way frequency table.

The athletic director of Springwood Middle School made a table to show how many of the students who play volleyball and basketball are in seventh and eighth grade.

	Volleyball	Basketball	Total
Seventh grade	9	17	26
Eighth grade	5	14	19
Total	14	31	45

Are there more basketball players in seventh or eighth grade?

_____

True or false: Overall, more seventh graders play these two sports compared to eighth graders.

_____

If one of the 45 student athletes is selected at random, what is the probability that the athlete is in seventh grade and plays volleyball? _____

A hairstylist notes the different hair appointments she has coming up.

	Adult	Child	Total
Color	12	1	13
Haircut	16	23	39
Total	28	24	52

What is the most common type of appointment?

_____

True or false: There are more adults than children with haircut appointments.

_____

What is the probability that a randomly selected appointment is for coloring hair? _____

Keep going! Answer each question using the data in the two-way frequency table.

Shaw's Diner has a popular sandwich and salad lunch special. Tuesday's orders are recorded below.

	House salad	Harvest salad	Total
Italian sub	14	6	20
Grilled cheese	18	25	43
Total	32	31	63

Which was the more popular sandwich on Tuesday: the Italian sub or the grilled cheese?

_____

True or false: Out of the customers who ordered the Italian sub, eight more customers ordered the house salad than the harvest salad.

_____

What is the probability that a randomly chosen customer ordered an Italian sub with a harvest salad? _____

During his shift, a ranger at Pinnacles National Park collected data on guest entries at the park entrance.

	Drive-in	Walk-in	Total
Annual pass	16	8	24
Day pass	47	5	52
Total	63	13	76

Which was more popular during this shift: the annual pass or the day pass?

_____

True or false: More walk-ins had an annual pass than a day pass.

_____

What is the probability that a randomly chosen guest did not drive in for entry? _____

Learn!

Two-way relative frequency tables show relative frequencies for two variables. A **relative frequency** describes the ratio of the number of times an event occurs to the total number of observations. You can calculate the relative frequency of an event by dividing its frequency by the total number of observations. Relative frequencies can be expressed as fractions, decimals, or percentages.

You can use a two-way frequency table to create a two-way relative frequency table.

For example, this frequency table shows the votes for snacks for a school's spring dance.

To make a relative frequency table, divide each entry by the total number of votes, 200.

Frequency table

	Chips	Cookies	Total
Seventh grade	54	34	88
Eighth grade	32	80	112
Total	86	114	200

Relative frequency table

	Chips	Cookies	Total
Seventh grade	$\frac{54}{200} = 0.27 = 27\%$	$\frac{34}{200} = 0.17 = 17\%$	$\frac{88}{200} = 0.44 = 44\%$
Eighth grade	$\frac{32}{200} = 0.16 = 16\%$	$\frac{80}{200} = 0.4 = 40\%$	$\frac{112}{200} = 0.56 = 56\%$
Total	$\frac{86}{200} = 0.43 = 43\%$	$\frac{114}{200} = 0.57 = 57\%$	$\frac{200}{200} = 1 = 100\%$

Make a two-way relative frequency table for each situation using the two-way frequency table. Write the relative frequencies as percents.

Christina sells necklace chains. She recorded the orders from the past month.

Frequency table

	16-inch	20-inch	Total
Gold	20	12	32
Silver	36	12	48
Total	56	24	80

Relative frequency table

	16-inch	20-inch	Total
Gold			
Silver			
Total			

The Adams Hill neighborhood is planning a new park. Some residents were surveyed about which location and kind of park they would prefer.

Frequency table

	Dog park	Skate park	Total
East side	8	5	13
West side	9	3	12
Total	17	8	25

Relative frequency table

	Dog park	Skate park	Total
East side			
West side			
Total			

Answer each question using the data in the two-way relative frequency table.

The students attending after-school programs at Mills Arts Center had the option of joining drama or orchestra. The arts director recorded the relative frequencies of their choices below.

	Drama	Orchestra	Total
Seventh grade	18%	20%	38%
Eighth grade	38%	24%	62%
Total	56%	44%	100%

What percent of students are seventh graders and in orchestra?

_____

True or false: More eighth graders are involved in drama than orchestra.

_____

What is the probability that a randomly selected student attending after-school programs is in drama? _____

Oakwood Middle School is having a movie-night fundraiser. Students were asked for their movie and snack preferences. The relative frequencies are recorded below.

	Popcorn	Cotton candy	Total
Prince of the River	0.08	0.13	0.21
Country of Mystery	0.35	0.44	0.79
Total	0.43	0.57	1

What percent of students prefer to watch *Prince of the River*?

_____

True or false: 44% of all the students prefer cotton candy over popcorn.

_____

The school decides to play the movie that most students preferred. Which movie did the school choose to play?

_____

Keep going! Answer each question using the data in the two-way relative frequency table.

Ms. Gilmore's math classes had the choice between making either a paper poster or a digital poster to show the results of their project. She recorded the relative frequencies of their choices below.

	Paper poster	Digital poster	Total
Period 1	26%	28%	54%
Period 2	32%	14%	46%
Total	58%	42%	100%

Which was the more popular option in period 1: a paper poster or a digital poster?

_____

Which was the more popular option in period 2: a paper poster or a digital poster?

_____

Which was the more popular option for both periods combined?

_____

The manager of the South Hills Recreation Center wants to know if visitors would prefer a roller-skating rink or a rock-climbing wall added to the center. She asks 100 visitors which they would prefer and records the results in a two-way relative frequency table.

	Skating rink	Climbing wall	Total
Adults	0.11	0.48	0.59
Youth	0.22	0.19	0.41
Total	0.33	0.67	1

Did the manager ask more adult visitors or more youth visitors?

_____

True or false: Twice as many youth visitors as adult visitors voted for the roller-skating rink.

_____

The manager decides to go with what more people prefer. What did the manager choose to add to the center?

_____

Challenge!

IXL.com
Checkpoint ID

HJG

202 Solving multi-step equations

Time for review! Solve each equation.

$4p + 28 = 6p$

$\frac{b}{10} + 4 = 11$

$7(k - 3) + 35 = 84$

$\frac{2}{3}r - 44 = 8r$

$9(n + 8) = 5n - 12$

$0.4d = 6 - 0.4d$

$2(a - 4) - a = 6(a + 7)$

$\frac{1}{3}v + \frac{5}{3}v - \frac{1}{2}v = 12$

$\frac{3}{4}(t - 3) + t = -\frac{5}{2}$

Challenge!

IXL.com
Checkpoint ID
BBZ

Solve each system of equations using any method.

$y = x + 16$
$y = 9x$

(_____ , _____)

$y = x$
$-27 = 10x - y$

(_____ , _____)

$y = x - 1$
$83 = 6x + 5y$

(_____ , _____)

$3x + 4y = -10$
$-2x - 4y = 20$

(_____ , _____)

$10x - 7y = 27$
$-5x + 14y = -24$

(_____ , _____)

$2x - 6y = -28$
$-11x - 18y = 1$

(_____ , _____)

The Museville Marching Band has a bake sale each year to raise money for new uniforms. This year, Erin is in charge of organizing the bake sale. Erin is looking at data from the previous years' bake sales. Determine whether the relationship shown in each table represents a function.

Money raised	Uniforms purchased
$240	2
$480	4
$1,200	10
$1,440	12

Bake sale duration (hr.)	Baked goods sold
2	60
2	72
3	150
5	215

Band size	Volunteers
60	15
64	15
75	15
82	15

function   not a function   function   not a function   function   not a function

Answer the following questions.

Erin is deciding whether to make brownies or lemon poppy seed muffins to bring to the bake sale this year. The total cost, c, to make b brownies is represented by the equation $c = 0.27b$. To make lemon poppy seed muffins, Erin first needs to buy a muffin pan for $8. After that, it costs $0.21 per muffin. So, the total cost to make m muffins is $c = 0.21m + 8$.

If Erin wants to make 36 baked goods, how much would that cost for each option?

Brownies: _____

Muffins: _____

If Erin wants to make 5 dozen baked goods, how much would that cost for each option?

Brownies: _____

Muffins: _____

After the bake sale, the Museville Marching Band will use the money raised to buy new uniforms. They need to decide whether to purchase uniforms from Band Essentials or Uniform Utopia. Answer the following questions.

Band Essentials charges the same amount for every uniform. The graph shows the cost of ordering certain numbers of uniforms.

What is the cost per uniform?

_____

Write an equation to represent the total cost, y, of ordering x uniforms.

_____

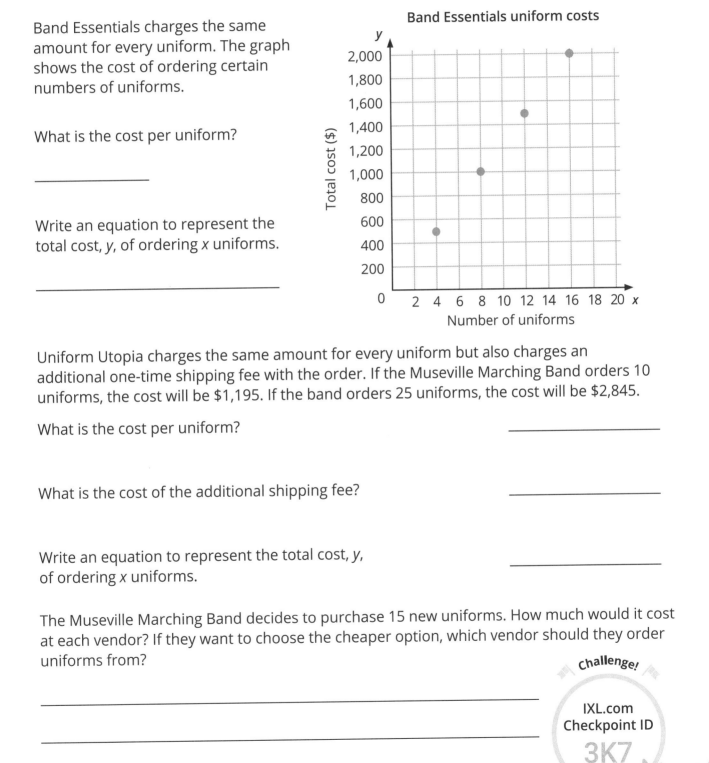

Band Essentials uniform costs

Uniform Utopia charges the same amount for every uniform but also charges an additional one-time shipping fee with the order. If the Museville Marching Band orders 10 uniforms, the cost will be $1,195. If the band orders 25 uniforms, the cost will be $2,845.

What is the cost per uniform?   _____

What is the cost of the additional shipping fee?   _____

Write an equation to represent the total cost, y,
of ordering x uniforms.   _____

The Museville Marching Band decides to purchase 15 new uniforms. How much would it cost at each vendor? If they want to choose the cheaper option, which vendor should they order uniforms from?

_____

_____

Challenge!

IXL.com
Checkpoint ID

3K7

Mr. Carino owns a coffee shop called Java Jupiter. He recently added a bookshelf, but he wants to rearrange the furniture to make better use of the space. Follow the directions below to help Mr. Carino determine a new layout for Java Jupiter.

Current layout

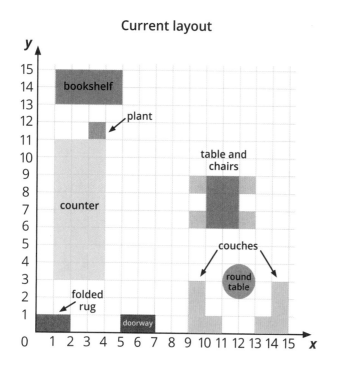

New layout

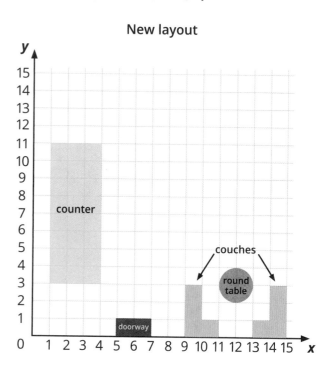

Mr. Carino wants to move the rectangular table and chairs farther away from the couches to spread out the guest seating. Draw the table and chairs on the new layout, and describe the transformation(s) that could map them from their old location to the new location.

_____

_____

_____

Mr. Carino wants to move the bookshelf closer to the guest seating. Draw the bookshelf on the new layout, and describe the transformation(s) that could map the bookshelf from its old location to the new location.

_____

_____

_____

Keep going! Follow the directions below to help Mr. Carino determine a new layout for Java Jupiter.

Mr. Carino likes the way his couches are arranged. Are the two couches similar, congruent, or neither? Explain how you know using one or more transformations.

_____

_____

_____

There is a rug in the corner of the coffee shop that is folded up. The rug unfolds to be twice its current width and length. Mr. Carino wants to unfold the rug and position it in front of the doorway. Draw the transformed rug on the new layout. Are the two regions covered by the folded rug and unfolded rug similar, congruent, or neither? Explain how you know using one or more transformations.

_____

_____

_____

Finally, when Mr. Carino is facing the counter, he notices that the plant to the right of it is hard to see when you walk into the coffee shop. He wants to move the plant to the opposite side of the counter so it's closer to the doorway. Draw the plant on the new layout, and describe the transformation(s) that could map the plant from its old location to the new location.

_____

_____

_____

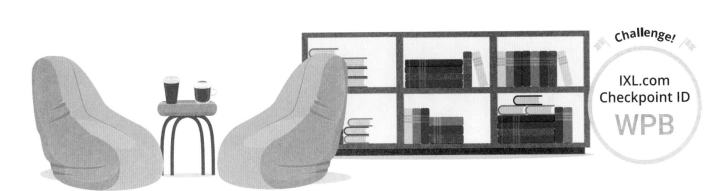

Rational numbers can be written in different ways. This answer key includes fractions and mixed numbers that are in simplest form. Keep in mind that there may be other equivalent answers that are also correct.

PAGE 4

5	3	2
1	8	7
10	9	6
12	15	13
14	20	18

PAGE 5

–7	11	±2
±20	–16	–12
17	–9	±19
±18	20	±15

PAGE 6

$a = ±4$	$w = ±11$	$m = ±6$
$y = ±10$	$z = ±7$	$k = ±15$
$c = ±13$	$p = ±16$	$b = ±14$
$s = ±\frac{4}{7}$	$n = ±\frac{5}{12}$	$g = ±\frac{3}{20}$
	$j = ±17$	$t = ±\frac{8}{19}$

PAGE 7

2	5	4
7	1	9
10	6	8
30	20	11
40	12	

PAGE 8

–2	10	–8
4	6	–9
–30	$-\frac{3}{5}$	–60
50	$\frac{11}{12}$	–70

$-\sqrt[3]{-8} = -(-2) = 2$

Explanations will vary. One possible explanation is shown below.

The answer changed from negative to positive.

PAGE 9

$z = 4$	$b = –1$	$d = 7$
$j = 12$	$p = –11$	$t = 5$
$w = 30$	$m = \frac{1}{7}$	$s = –60$
$a = -\frac{3}{8}$	$y = –80$	$f = -\frac{9}{10}$
$q = \frac{4}{11}$	$r = –100$	

PAGE 10

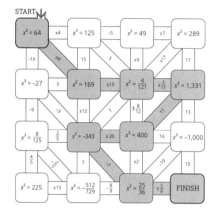

PAGE 11

0.4	0.375	$-0.1\overline{6}$
$0.\overline{18}$	–2.15	$-1.\overline{7}$
4.75	$4.41\overline{6}$	$-2.\overline{3}$
–1.525		

PAGE 12

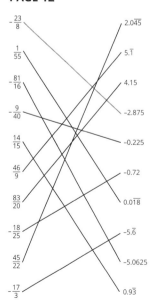

PAGE 13

$\frac{1}{11}$ $\frac{7}{9}$ $\frac{4}{11}$

PAGE 14

$\frac{4}{15}$ $\frac{4}{45}$ $1\frac{5}{9}$

PAGE 15

natural number	integer
whole number	irrational number
natural number	irrational number
integer	rational number
irrational number	

PAGE 16

$\frac{5}{6}$	–35	$-\sqrt{11}$	–51.8
π	$\sqrt{100}$	$\sqrt[3]{6}$	$10.\overline{24}$
$-8.\overline{6}$	0.125	$\sqrt{42}$	150,326
0	$-\sqrt{20}$	$-\sqrt{2}$	$\sqrt[3]{64}$
$-\frac{1}{4}$	$\frac{10}{2}$	–π	$\sqrt{3}$
4π	$\sqrt{25} - 99.7$	$-\sqrt{36} + \sqrt{1}$	$3\frac{2}{11}$
$\frac{77}{\sqrt[3]{343}}$	$-\sqrt{5}$	$-\sqrt[3]{4}$	–4.8
312.5	$-\frac{16}{3} + π$	$\sqrt{5}$	0.3

PAGE 17

2 and 3	9 and 10
5 and 6	1 and 2
3 and 4	11 and 12
8 and 9	3 and 4
9 and 10	4 and 5
5 and 6	7 and 8
10 and 11	

PAGE 18

PAGE 19

1 and 2	3 and 4
7 and 8	3 and 4
9 and 10	9 and 10
2 and 3	8 and 9
1 and 2	6 and 7
9 and 10	5 and 6
3.4 and 3.5	

PAGE 20

$5 + \sqrt{33}$

10 10.1 10.2 10.3 10.4 10.5 10.6 10.7 10.8 10.9 11

$\sqrt[3]{95}$

4 4.1 4.2 4.3 4.4 4.5 4.6 4.7 4.8 4.9 5

$\sqrt{103} - 2$

8 8.1 8.2 8.3 8.4 8.5 8.6 8.7 8.8 8.9 9

$3 + \sqrt{75}$

11 11.1 11.2 11.3 11.4 11.5 11.6 11.7 11.8 11.9 12

$\sqrt[3]{24}$

2 2.1 2.2 2.3 2.4 2.5 2.6 2.7 2.8 2.9 3

$\sqrt[3]{228}$

6 6.1 6.2 6.3 6.4 6.5 6.6 6.7 6.8 6.9 7

PAGE 21

$\sqrt{18} < 5.\overline{3}$ $4\frac{1}{3} < \sqrt{40}$

$\pi < \frac{10}{2}$ $8.48 < \sqrt[3]{750}$

$-\frac{9}{4} > -\pi$ $\sqrt{50} - 5 > 1.\overline{81}$

$-\sqrt{2} < -0.99$ $\sqrt[3]{-11} < -\frac{11}{6}$

$7.63 > 2\pi$ $8\frac{1}{5} - \frac{4}{5} < \sqrt{65}$

$100 - \sqrt[3]{814} > 90.\overline{1}$ $-\sqrt{30} < 2 -7.38$

PAGE 22

$\sqrt{-9} = \sqrt{(9)(-1)}$
$\quad = \sqrt{9} \cdot \sqrt{-1}$
$\quad = 3 \cdot \sqrt{-1}$
$\quad = 3i$

So, $\sqrt{-9} = 3i$.

PAGE 23

$\sqrt{-36} = \sqrt{(36)(-1)}$
$\quad = \sqrt{36} \cdot \sqrt{-1}$
$\quad = 6 \cdot \sqrt{-1}$
$\quad = 6i$

So, $\sqrt{-36} = 6i$.

PAGE 23, continued

$\sqrt{-64} = \sqrt{(64)(-1)}$
$\quad = \sqrt{64} \cdot \sqrt{-1}$
$\quad = 8 \cdot \sqrt{-1}$
$\quad = 8i$

So, $\sqrt{-64} = 8i$.

PAGE 24

8	1,296	–9
–64	160,000	–125
256	1,000	49
–125,000	$\frac{1}{9}$	–6,561
	$\frac{4}{49}$	–12.25

PAGE 25

5^{10}	8^7	9^{15}
$(-4)^7$	$\left(\frac{2}{3}\right)^8$	10.25^9
$6^5 \cdot 4^5$	$10^7 \cdot 2^7$	
$3^8 \cdot 2.6^8$	$6^3 \cdot (-7)^3$	
$\left(-\frac{3}{5}\right)^2 \cdot \left(2\frac{1}{4}\right)^2$		

PAGE 26

6^{21}	3^{20}	20^{16}
10^{16}	8^{10}	12^{18}
2^{70}	4^{24}	9^{60}
15^{24}	7^{56}	5^{99}
0.9^{12}	18^{120}	11^{10}
13^{36}	0.23^{48}	4.18^{36}
	25^{35}	0.09^{44}

PAGE 27

3^8	9^3	5^5
12^7	6^6	2^4
8^8	10^3	4^5
15^{10}	0.8^{12}	30^4
$(-4)^7$	80^6	12.65^3
7^3	$(-11)^8$	

PAGE 28

$\frac{1}{2^5}$	$\frac{1}{9^3}$	1
$\frac{1}{3^8}$	1	1
$\frac{1}{20^6}$	1	$\frac{1}{11^4}$
1	1	$\frac{1}{19^2}$
$\frac{1}{83^7}$	$\frac{1}{(-10)^{10}}$	–1
	1	$\frac{1}{999^3}$

PAGE 29

$1 = \frac{n^3}{n^3} = n^{\boxed{3}-\boxed{3}} = n^{\boxed{0}}$

$1 = n^0$

$\frac{1}{n^4} = \frac{n^0}{n^4} = n^{\boxed{0}-\boxed{4}} = n^{\boxed{-4}}$

$\frac{1}{n^4} = n^{-4}$

PAGE 30

3^{13}	8^{12}	0.03^5
$\frac{1}{9^2}$	4.2^{21}	$(-14)^{10}$
4.5^6	11^{20}	5.127^{12}
3^2	$\frac{1}{(-2)^8}$	$(-12)^9$
9^7	$\left(\frac{1}{7}\right)^7$	$\frac{1}{(-35)^6}$
9.17^{16}	$\frac{1}{(-12)^7}$	$(-6.87)^9$

Answer key

PAGE 31

8^0
(−10)^{10}
8^4 · 8^5
17^8
17^{-6}
8^{10}
(−10)^5 · (−10)^5
$\frac{1}{(-10)^4}$
(8^5)^4
(−10)^9
17^3 · 17^5
8^9
(−10)$^{-4}$
17^{15}
$\frac{17^{11}}{17^5}$
17^6
$\frac{(-10)^{17}}{(-10)^8}$
1
(17^5)^3
8^{20}
$\frac{8^{12}}{8^2}$
$\frac{1}{17^6}$

PAGE 32

5^{16} $\frac{1}{8^5}$

$(-7)^3$ $(-20)^{11}$

$\frac{1}{11^{15}}$ 8.12^{12}

0.38^4 45^{16}

2.5^{20} $\frac{1}{(-9)^9}$

PAGE 33

4×10^5
2×10^{-5}
2×10^8
3×10^{-8}

PAGE 34

430,000   0.0091
70,000,000   0.0002
0.0000000055   670,000,000
0.00000003   960,000
4,450,000   0.000000703

PAGE 35

9×10^6 8.3×10^{-7}
6.5×10^7 4×10^{-3}

PAGE 35, continued

8×10^{-8} 2.2×10^8
1×10^9 2.031×10^{-6}
4.1×10^{-11} 5.07×10^{10}

PAGE 36

0.000000005 3×10^{-5}
130,000,000   70,000,000,000
7×10^7 5.5×10^{-8}
8×10^5 0.0000087
30,000,000 3.6×10^8
4,360,000 6.1×10^{-9}
1.75×10^9 0.00000076
0.000000022 1.5×10^6

PAGE 37

$0.00006 < 6 \times 10^{-4}$
$8.4 \times 10^7 > 8,400,000$

$0.00000075 > 7.5 \times 10^{-8}$
$9.92 \times 10^{-6} = 0.00000992$

$5 \times 10^9 > 500,000,000$
$63,000,000 > 6.3 \times 10^6$

$0.000000013 > 1.3 \times 10^{-10}$
$4.48 \times 10^4 = 44,800$

$0.00000000877 = 8.77 \times 10^{-9}$
$3.9 \times 10^8 < 39,000,000,000$

$2.5 \times 10^{-3} > 0.00025$
$0.0000072 > 7.2 \times 10^{-7}$

$115,000,000,000 < 1.15 \times 10^{12}$
$3.65 \times 10^{-6} < 0.0000365$

$4 \times 10^8 > 6 \times 10^7$
$5.89 \times 10^{10} < 589,000,000,000$

PAGE 38

ants on Earth

grain of sugar

mitochondria
chloroplast
nucleus

fossil C
fossil B
fossil A
fossil D

PAGE 39

3.1×10^3 8.7×10^8
2.3×10^{-7} 6.8×10^{10}
1.039×10^{-4} 4.3×10^{-9}
1.63×10^7 3.3×10^{-7}
1.4956×10^{-9} 5.25×10^8

PAGE 40

2.2×10^6 6.29×10^5
3.89×10^{-6} 6.67×10^{-9}
5.0267×10^{10} 4.022×10^6
    8.843×10^{-8}

PAGE 41

8×10^4 8.76×10^{10}
4.667×10^{-7} 1.02×10^9
8.449×10^6 1.4326×10^{-4}
1.35×10^{-7} 4.804×10^{10}
1.83×10^{11} 1.3175×10^{-4}
9×10^{-9} 1.8115×10^{-8}

PAGE 42

4.32×10^{11} 6.9×10^{14}
3.15×10^{12} 8.84×10^{18}
3.216×10^{-2} 1.176×10^{-9}
    2.265×10^{-1}

PAGE 43

1.12×10^4 3.14×10^6
1.95×10^5 3.5×10^5
1.425×10^{-3} 4.25×10^8
9.5×10^{-14}

PAGE 44

4.192×10^5 6.3×10^4
2.318×10^{13} 3.25×10^{-6}
7.728×10^{-6} 1.436×10^{-8}
2.1652×10^8 5.8×10^{-8}
1.596×10^{-3} 9.0627×10^7

PAGE 45

3.825×10^5
1.95×10^3
7.425×10^3
2.37×10^{-4}

PAGE 46

$h = 3$	$d = 6$	$p = -2$
$c = -2$	$y = 2$	$b = -3$
$r = 3$	$s = 11$	$n = 4.4$
$m = -2.4$	$z = -6$	$u = 16$
	$j = \frac{10}{3}$	$a = 12$

PAGE 47

$b = 2$	$q = 3$	$s = -2$
$x = -15$	$y = 11$	$u = \frac{12}{7}$
$t = 4.2$	$p = 40$	

PAGE 48

$w = 3$	$s = 1$	$y = -5$
	$c = 12$	$b = 6$

PAGE 49

$z = 7$	$k = 3$	$b = 3$
$m = 5$	$q = 3$	$s = -36$
$d = -\frac{4}{3}$	$t = 4.5$	$j = -13.5$
$c = 7$	$p = 68$	

PAGE 50

$g = 4$	$f = -8$	$k = -3$
$x = 0$	$b = \frac{2}{3}$	$u = -1.5$

PAGE 51

$g = 5$	$y = -4$	$x = 2$
$m = -3$	$t = \frac{5}{4}$	$n = -2$
$f = -\frac{10}{3}$	$w = 2.2$	$j = \frac{3}{2}$
$c = 1.4$	$a = \frac{13}{12}$	

PAGE 52

$w = 6$	$y = -12$	$d = 6$
$g = 5$	$t = 2$	$p = -2$
$v = 7$	$b = 16$	$a = -4$
	$n = -5$	$q = 0$

PAGE 53

$a = 12$	$v = -5$	$n = -11$
$x = 8$	$s = -3$	$z = 18$
$m = 1$	$b = 1.9$	$p = -8$
$w = 2.9$	$t = \frac{4}{5}$	

PAGE 54

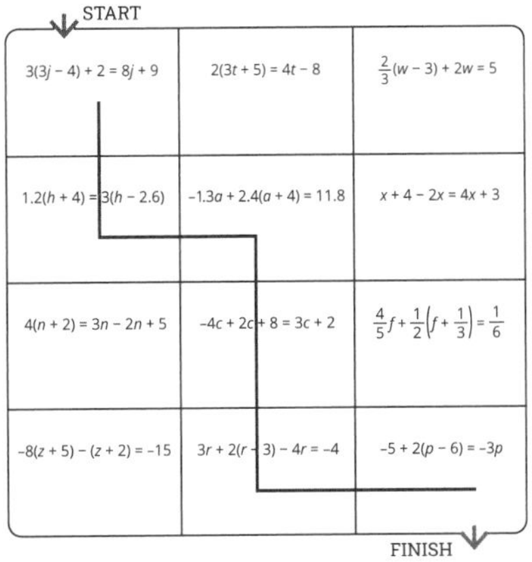

PAGE 55

4 T-shirts
9 people
1.25 hours
$11

PAGE 56

one solution
infinitely many solutions
no solution

PAGE 57

one solution
one solution
infinitely many solutions
no solution
infinitely many solutions
one solution
no solution
infinitely many solutions
infinitely many solutions
no solution

PAGE 58

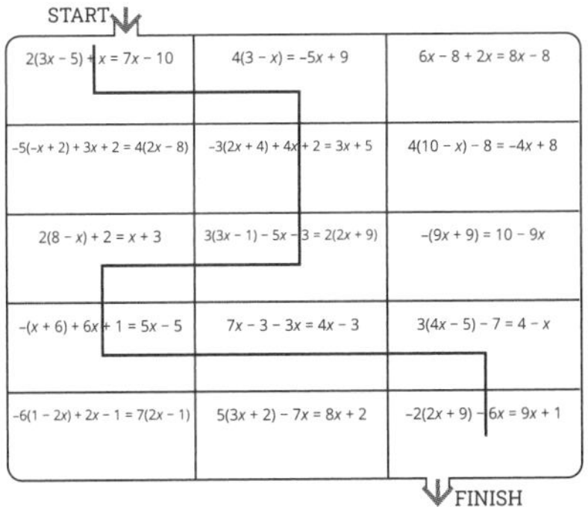

PAGE 59

$10x + 4 = 10x + 4$
$3x - 9 = 3x - 9$
$-5x + 6 = -5x + 6$
$-4x + 10 = 10 - 4x$
$7x = 3x + 4x$
$8x - 6 - 2x = 6x - 6$

$4x = 4x + 9$
$8x - 4 = 8x + 2$
$6x + 1 - 2x = 4x + 3$
$2(-3x + 5) = 1 - 6x$

Answers may vary. Some possible answers are shown below.

$-x + 6 + 3x = 2x + 1$
$-x + 5 = 3x - 4x$

Equations may vary. Some possible equations are shown below.

$-x + 6 + 3x = 2x + 6$
$-x + 0 = 3x - 4x$

PAGE 60

$y = 4x$	$y = \frac{1}{3}x$
$y = 2x$	$y = \frac{3}{2}x$
$y = \frac{1}{5}x$	$y = \frac{3}{5}x$
	$y = \frac{4}{3}x$

PAGE 61

$y = \frac{1}{2}x$	$y = 3x$
$y = \frac{2}{5}x$	$y = 4x$

PAGE 62

$2.50 $1.50

cheddar

45   50

Mya

PAGE 63

$12 $13

paddleboard

1.5   2.5

graduation cap cookie

PAGE 64

2                    $\frac{1}{3}$

PAGE 65

$\frac{3}{4}$ 5

1                    $\frac{2}{5}$

Explanations will vary. One possible explanation is shown below.

The constant of proportionality is the same as the slope.

PAGE 66

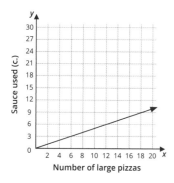

Slope = $\frac{1}{2}$

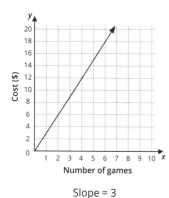

Slope = 3

PAGE 66, *continued*

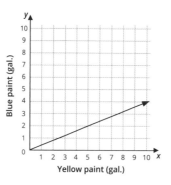

Slope = $\frac{2}{5}$

PAGE 68

zero   positive

4

negative   undefined

$-\frac{1}{2}$

PAGE 69

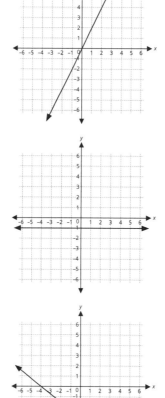

PAGE 69, *continued*

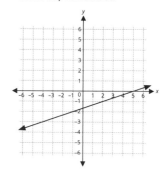

PAGE 70

$m = -2$ $m = 5$ $m = 0$

$m = \frac{1}{2}$ $m = -4$ $m = -\frac{2}{3}$

PAGE 71

$m = 3$ $m = \frac{1}{4}$ $m = -3$

$m = -\frac{1}{3}$ $m = 8$ $m = \frac{4}{3}$

$m = -\frac{7}{2}$ $m = -7$ $m = \frac{3}{5}$

$m = 4$ $m = -\frac{4}{3}$ $m = -\frac{9}{8}$

PAGE 72

(6, 3)

(2, –4)

(0, –7)

(–1, –6)

PAGE 73

$b = 4$ $b = -2$

Slope = 1   Slope = $-\frac{1}{3}$

PAGE 74

$m = -2$ $m = \frac{1}{3}$ $m = 4$

$b = 5$ $b = 8$ $b = -3$

$m = -\frac{1}{2}$ $m = 3$ $m = -1$

$b = -1$ $b = 2$ $b = 6$

$y = 2x + 4$ $y = -3x + 1$

$y = \frac{2}{3}x - 7$ $y = \frac{4}{3}x$

$y = x - 2$

PAGE 75

$m = -2$ $\qquad$ $b = 2$

$\qquad$ $y = -2x + 2$

$m = 3$ $\qquad$ $b = -4$

$\qquad$ $y = 3x - 4$

PAGE 76

$y = -\frac{1}{3}x + 3$ $\qquad$ $y = \frac{2}{3}x$

$y = x + 3$ $\qquad$ $y = -\frac{3}{2}x + 4$

PAGE 77

$m = 2$

$b = -3$

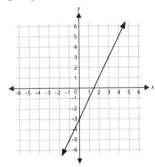

$m = -\frac{1}{4}$

$b = 1$

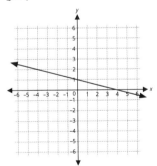

PAGE 78

$y = -3x + 4$

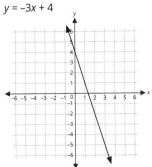

PAGE 78, *continued*

$y = \frac{5}{2}x - 2$

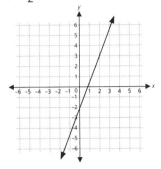

$y = \frac{2}{3}x + 1$

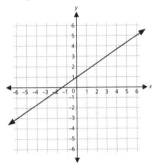

$y = -x + 3$

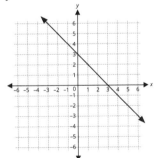

PAGE 79

$5x - y = 4$

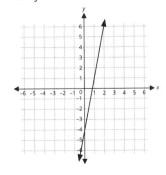

PAGE 79, *continued*

$x - 4y = 12$

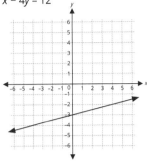

PAGE 80

$2x + 3y = 9$

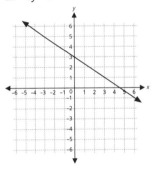

$3x + 2y = -6$

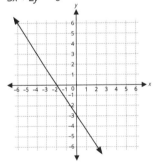

$4x + 3y = 6$

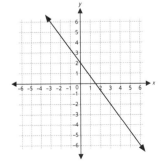

PAGE 80, *continued*

$x - 4y = 0$

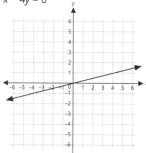

PAGE 81

$y = 1$

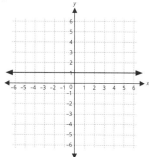

$x = -4$

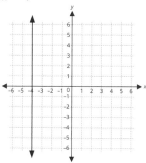

PAGE 82

$y = 2x + 9$ $y = -4x + 24$

$y = \frac{1}{2}x + 3$ $y = 2x - 5$

PAGE 83

$y = 4x - 20$ $y = \frac{3}{5}x + 1$

$y = -x + 20$ $y = -3x + 15$

$y = \frac{1}{4}x - 10$ $y = -\frac{4}{3}x + 4$

PAGE 84

$y = 5x - 6$ $y = -2x + 4$

$y = \frac{3}{4}x + 3$ $y = -\frac{5}{2}x + 5$

PAGE 85

$y = -x + 7$ $y = \frac{2}{5}x + 2$

$y = 3x - 8$ $y = -\frac{1}{2}x - 3$

$y = -8x + 8$ $y = \frac{7}{10}x - 30$

$y = -\frac{2}{3}x + 5$ $y = -4x + 12$

PAGE 86

$y = 8x - 12$ $y = -2x + 6$

$y = \frac{1}{4}x + 4$ $y = -\frac{1}{3}x - 7$

PAGE 87

$y = \frac{1}{5}x - 2$ $y = 5x + 1$

$y = 6x - 6$ $y = \frac{7}{8}x - 8$

$y = 8$ $y = -x - 3$

$y = -8x + 3$

PAGE 88

$-\frac{2}{3}$ $-\frac{1}{2}$

                    -4

                    $\frac{5}{2}$

PAGE 89

-5 $\frac{3}{5}$

$-\frac{1}{2}$ -3

$y = \frac{1}{3}x + 4$ $y = \frac{1}{6}x + 1$

PAGE 90

The one-time joining fee is $40.

The monthly membership fee is $20.

$y = 20x + 40$

Quinn started with 50 cayenne peppers in the basket.

Quinn uses 4 cayenne peppers for every jar of hot sauce she makes.

$y = -4x + 50$

PAGE 91

$y = 12x + 4$

$y = -1.5x + 40$

PAGE 91, *continued*

$y = 10x + 45$

$y = -4x + 350$

$y = 0.75x + 30$

PAGE 92

$y = 15x + 5$ $65

$y = -3x + 36$ 12

$y = -2x + 28$ 14

$y = -4.5x + 20$ 2

PAGE 93

$20 $75

$y = 20x + 75$ 4

$\frac{1}{4}$ 50

$y = -\frac{1}{4}x + 50$ 25

PAGE 95

one solution

infinitely many solutions

no solution

infinitely many solutions

one solution

no solution

infinitely many solutions

one solution

no solution

infinitely many solutions

Explanations will vary. One possible explanation is shown below.

Yes, both of the equations are true when $x = 1$ and $y = 7$.

PAGE 96

$y = -x + 4$ $y = 2x - 5$

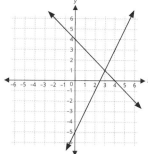

(3, 1)

215

PAGE 96, *continued*

$y = x - 1$ $y = 3x + 5$

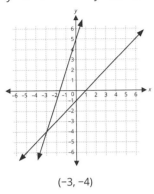

(−3, −4)

PAGE 97

$y = \frac{1}{2}x - 2$ $y = -\frac{1}{4}x + 1$

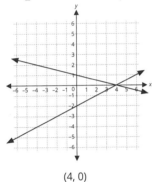

(4, 0)

$2y = x + 6$ $x + y = -3$

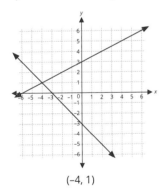

(−4, 1)

PAGE 97, *continued*

$3y = 9 - 3x$ $y = \frac{2}{3}x - 2$

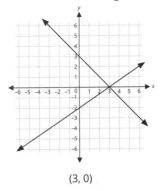

(3, 0)

PAGE 98

(1, 2)   (−4, 1)

PAGE 99

(2, 6)   (−4, −4)
(−3, −5)   (2, −6)
(2, 2)   (0, 3)

PAGE 100

(−1, 3)   (2, 2)

PAGE 101

(2, 5)   (−3, −1)
(2, −3)   (4, 4)
(0, 4)   (2, 2)
(2, −5)

PAGE 102

(3, 5)   (−4, 0)
(−2, −7)   (1, −1)
(3, −9)   (−4, 5)
          (−4, 7)

PAGE 103

It was TOO CUBED!

PAGE 104

$y = 10x + 55$
$y = 8x + 65$
It will take 5 weeks. They will each have $105.

$2x + 3y = 34$
$4x + y = 28$
Tamara uses 5 peaches for each crisp. She uses 8 peaches for each pie.

PAGE 104, *continued*

$3x + 5y = 290$
$2x + 6y = 300$
Each bag of cat food weighs 30 pounds. Each bag of dog food weighs 40 pounds.

PAGE 105

$8x + 12y = 1,020$
$x + y = 120$
There are 105 students and 15 chaperones on the field trip.

$x + y = 15$
$2x + 3y = 39$
There are 6 little blue penguins and 9 Adélie penguins.

$4x + 3y = 449$
$x + y = 120$
There were 89 people who attended the sea lion show. There were 31 people who watched the 3D movie.

PAGE 106

not a function   function

PAGE 107

function   not a function
function   function
not a function   not a function

PAGE 108

Answers will vary. Some possible answers are shown below.

(10, 4)   (18, 2)

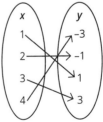

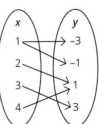

PAGE 108, *continued*

Answers will vary. Some possible answers are shown below.

x	y
3	4
7	–2
15	3
11	5

x	y
3	4
7	–2
15	3
15	6

PAGE 109

not a function

The *x*-value –2 has two different *y*-values. So, this is not a function.

function

Each *x*-value has exactly one *y*-value. So, this is a function.

not a function

The *x*-value 3 has two different *y*-values. So, this is not a function.

PAGE 110

2   3

    Function Q

$\frac{3}{4}$ 1

    Function S

$\frac{5}{2}$ 3

    Function B

PAGE 111

1   3

    Function U

1   0

    Function C

3   4

    Function K

PAGE 112

$c = \frac{2}{5}t + 2$

$g = -2b + 24$

$h = \frac{2,000}{3}t + 8,000$

PAGE 113

$c = 13p + 50$

$13

$p = 21h + 450$

$450

$w = 100t + 50$

100

PAGE 114

nonlinear   linear

PAGE 115

linear	nonlinear	linear
linear	nonlinear	nonlinear
nonlinear	linear	nonlinear

PAGE 116

Prize 1	
Day	**Total money**
1	$1,000
2	$2,000
3	$3,000
4	$4,000
5	$5,000
6	$6,000
7	$7,000
8	$8,000
9	$9,000
10	$10,000
11	$11,000
12	$12,000
13	$13,000
14	$14,000
15	$15,000

PAGE 116, *continued*

Prize 2	
Day	**Total money**
1	$2
2	$4
3	$8
4	$16
5	$32
6	$64
7	$128
8	$256
9	$512
10	$1,024
11	$2,048
12	$4,096
13	$8,192
14	$16,384
15	$32,768

PAGE 117

Days 1 – 13

Days 14 – 15

Prize 1

$y = 1,000x$

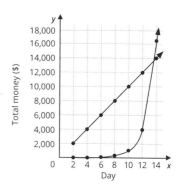

Answers will vary. A possible answer is shown.

The better prize is prize 2. The amount I earn from prize 2 grows faster and faster as the days go by. I would earn less money from prize 2 than prize 1 for the first 14 days. But after that, I would earn more money by choosing prize 2.

PAGE 118

Interval 1: constant

Interval 2: decreasing

Interval 3: increasing

PAGE 118, *continued*

Interval 1: decreasing

Interval 2: increasing

Interval 3: constant

Interval 4: decreasing

PAGE 119

B

E

D

A

F

C

PAGE 120

Graphs may vary. Possible answers are shown below.

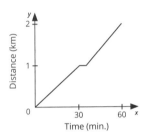

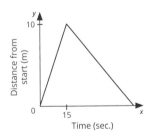

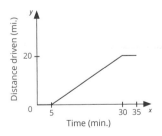

PAGE 120, *continued*

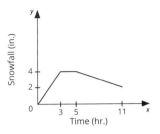

PAGE 121

10 kilometers

10 minutes

Explanations will vary. One possible explanation is shown below.

Vivian ran faster after taking a break. The slope of the graph is steeper after the break.

600 feet

6 hours

160 feet per hour

PAGE 122

reflection   rotation

translation

PAGE 123

translation   reflection

reflection   translation

rotation   translation

rotation   reflection

PAGE 124

ΔFGH was translated 2 units left and 4 units down to form ΔF'G'H'.

Quadrilateral *JKLM* was translated 8 units right and 3 units up to form quadrilateral *J'K'L'M'*.

F(3, 4) *F'*(1, 0)

Explanations will vary. One possible explanation is shown below.

The *x*-coordinate changes from 3 to 1, so it decreases by 2. The *y*-coordinate changes from 4 to 0, so it decreases by 4. When the triangle moves 2 units to the left, 2 is subtracted from the *x*-coordinate. When the triangle moves 4 units down, 4 is subtracted from the *y*-coordinate.

PAGE 125

S'(–4, 8) *T'*(–2, 6) *U'*(–4, 4)

J'(–4, –1) *K'*(1, –1) *L'*(–5, –4) *M'*(0, –4)

PAGE 126

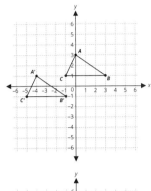

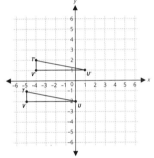

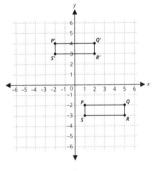

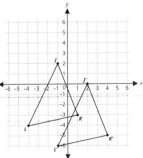

PAGE 127

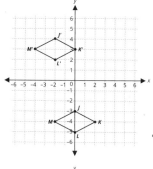

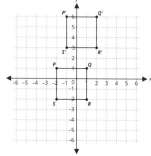

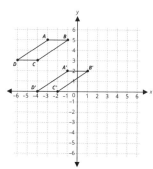

PAGE 128

Trapezoid *WXYZ* was reflected across the line *y* = 3 to form trapezoid *W'X'Y'Z'*.

△*PQR* was reflected across the *y*-axis to form △*P'Q'R'*.

P(3, −2) *P'*(−3, −2)

Explanations will vary. One possible explanation is shown below.

The *x*-coordinate of vertex *P* is 3, and the *x*-coordinate of vertex *P'* is −3. The *y*-coordinate of vertex *P* is −2, which is the same as the *y*-coordinate of vertex *P'*. The reflection of a point over the *y*-axis changes the *x*-coordinate to its opposite.

PAGE 129

Q'(5, −4) *R'*(4, −2) *S'*(−1, −1)
D'(−3, 2) *E'*(−6, 3) *F'*(−6, 0) *G'*(−3, −1)

PAGE 130

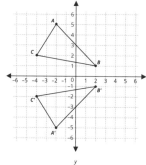

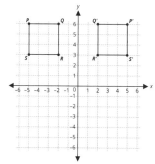

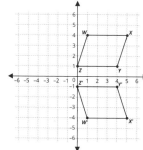

PAGE 131

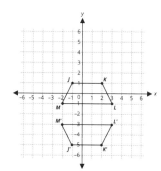

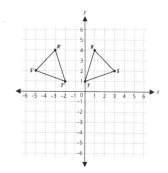

PAGE 131, *continued*

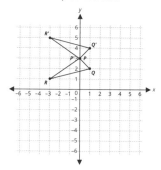

PAGE 132

△*QRS* was rotated 180° counterclockwise around the origin to form △*Q'R'S'*.

Parallelogram *DEFG* was rotated 90° counterclockwise around the origin to form parallelogram *D'E'F'G'*.

Q(−3, 4) *Q'*(3, −4)

Explanations will vary. One possible explanation is shown below.

Each coordinate changes by becoming its opposite. Rotating a figure 180° is the same as reflecting the figure over the *x*-axis and then over the *y*-axis. The reflection over the *x*-axis changes the *y*-coordinate to its opposite. The reflection over the *y*-axis changes the *x*-coordinate to its opposite.

PAGE 133

V'(0, −4) *W'*(−5, −6) *X'*(−4, −2)
J'(3, 2) *K'*(1, 2) *L'*(1, 5) *M'*(4, 5)

PAGE 134

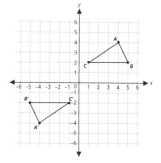

PAGE 134, *continued*

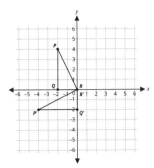

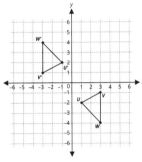

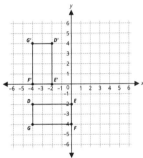

PAGE 135

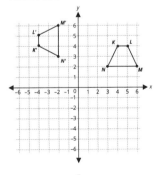

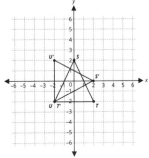

PAGE 135, *continued*

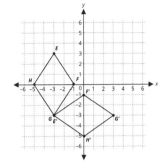

PAGE 136

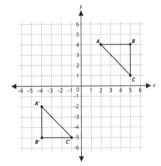

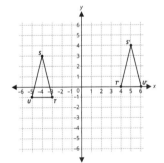

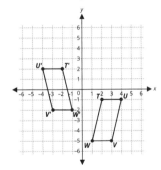

PAGE 137

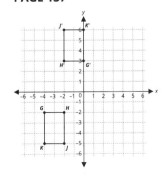

PAGE 137, *continued*

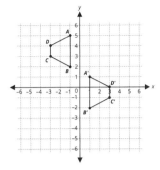

Explanations may vary. One possible explanation is shown below.

The area of rectangle *GHJK* is 6 square units, and the area of its image *G'H'J'K'* is 6 square units. The areas are the same.

PAGE 138

Explanations will vary. Some possible explanations are shown below.

The figures are congruent. A rotation 180° counterclockwise around the origin and a translation 1 unit left and 1 unit up will map figure *A* onto figure *B*.

The figures are not congruent. You cannot map one figure onto the other using a sequence of translations, reflections, and rotations.

PAGE 139

Explanations will vary. Some possible explanations are shown below

The figures are not congruent. You cannot map one figure onto the other using a sequence of translations, reflections, and rotations.

The figures are congruent. A rotation 90° counterclockwise around the origin and reflection across the *y*-axis will map figure *A* onto figure *B*.

The figures are congruent. A reflection across the *x*-axis and a translation 6 units left will map figure *A* onto figure *B*.

PAGE 141

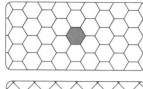

PAGE 142

ΔFGH was dilated from the origin by a scale factor of 2 to form $\Delta F'H'J'$.

Rectangle *STUV* was dilated from the origin by a scale factor of $\frac{1}{3}$ to form rectangle *S'T'U'V'*.

$G(3, -1)$ $G'(6, -2)$

Explanations will vary. One possible explanation is shown below.

The coordinates of vertex *G* have been multiplied by 2 to get the coordinates of vertex *G'*. This is because the triangle was dilated from the origin by a scale factor of 2.

PAGE 143

$D'(0, 4)$ $E'(8, 4)$ $F'(4, -12)$ $G'(-4, -12)$

$V'(-2, -1)$ $W'(0, -1)$ $X'(1, 2)$

PAGE 144

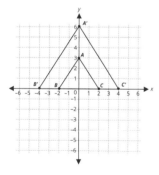

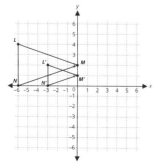

PAGE 144, *continued*

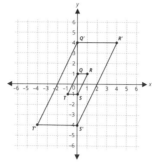

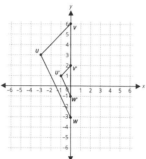

PAGE 145

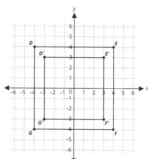

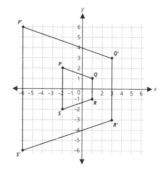

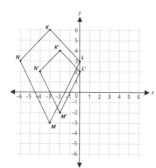

PAGE 146

Explanations will vary. One possible explanation is shown below.

The figures are not similar. You cannot map one figure onto the other using a sequence of transformations.

The figures are similar. A dilation from the origin by a scale factor of 2 and then a translation 6 units down will map figure *A* onto figure *B*.

PAGE 147

Explanations will vary. Some possible explanations are shown below.

The figures are not similar. You cannot map one figure onto the other using a sequence of transformations.

The figures are similar. A dilation from the origin by a scale factor of $\frac{1}{3}$ and then a reflection across the *x*-axis will map figure *A* onto figure *B*.

The figures are similar. A dilation from the origin by a scale factor of 2 and then a rotation 90° counterclockwise around the origin will map figure *A* onto figure *B*.

PAGE 148

Triangle	Length of vertical side	Length of horizontal side	Length of vertical side ÷ Length of horizontal side
ΔABC	6	3	2
ΔCDE	4	2	2
ΔEFG	2	1	2

PAGE 149

3

30

$\frac{1}{2}$

24

PAGE 150

$t = 80$ $d = 40$

$r = 39$ $x = 51$

           $y = 8$

PAGE 151

Answers may vary. Some possible answers are shown below

∠2 and ∠6

∠2 and ∠7

∠1 and ∠8

∠2 and ∠5

∠3 and ∠6

PAGE 152

$m\angle 1 = 85°$ $m\angle 5 = 95°$

$m\angle 2 = 95°$ $m\angle 6 = 85°$

$m\angle 3 = 85°$ $m\angle 7 = 95°$

$m\angle 4 = 85°$

Explanations will vary. Some possible explanations are shown below.

∠5 and the given angle are alternate exterior angles, so they must be congruent.

∠7 and the given angle are corresponding angles, so they must be congruent.

$m\angle 1 = 109°$ $m\angle 5 = 71°$

$m\angle 2 = 71°$ $m\angle 6 = 109°$

$m\angle 3 = 109°$ $m\angle 7 = 71°$

$m\angle 4 = 109°$

Explanations will vary. One possible explanation is shown below.

∠6 and the given angle are same-side interior angles, so they must be supplementary. 180 − 71 = 109.

PAGE 153

$x = 12$ $c = 13$

$y = 25$ $d = 5$

$m = 24$ $g = 24$

$n = 3$ $h = 11$

PAGE 154

$p = 25$ $x = 30$

$c = 48$ $n = 54$

PAGE 155

$a = 63.7$ $k = 43$

$v = 19$ $e = 88.3$

$y = 123.6$ $j = 25.7$

PAGE 156

$x = 10$ $g = 5$

$w = 50$ $c = 28$

$m = 3$ $d = 9$

PAGE 157

∠1 and ∠4

∠3 and ∠5

$m\angle 4 = m\angle 1$ $m\angle 5 = m\angle 3$

$m\angle 4 + m\angle 2 + m\angle 5 = 180°$

$m\angle 1 + m\angle 2 + m\angle 3 = 180°$

PAGE 158

$z = 120$ $a = 110$

$e = 87$ $q = 145$

PAGE 159

$b = 73.4$ $k = 119$

$r = 139.92$ $d = 123.6$

$y = 160.1$ $j = 154.15$

PAGE 160

$r = 10$ $g = 35$

$a = 12$ $n = 24$

$b = 8$ $y = 2$

PAGE 161

$z = 18$ $v = 12$

$q = 31$ $c = 4$

$f = 7$ $m = 11$

PAGE 162

97°

33°

84°

13

4

PAGE 163

$x = 10$

The measures of the angles of ΔLMN are 42°, 94°, and 44°.

$k = 17$

The measures of the angles of ΔQRS are 70°, 25°, and 85°.

PAGE 164

$c = 5$ cm $c = 13$ mi.

$c = 25$ ft. $c = 15$ mm

PAGE 165

$c = 20$ yd. $c = 30$ m

$c = 17$ km $c = 12.2$ in.

$c = 13.5$ cm $c = 7.1$ ft.

PAGE 166

$a = 3$ mi. $a = 15$ cm

$b = 9$ m $b = 6$ yd.

$a = 20$ in. $b = 24$ ft.

PAGE 167

$a = 12$ mm $b = 2$ yd.

$b = 4.6$ km $a = 5.7$ ft.

$a = 8.1$ cm $b = 19.2$ in.

PAGE 168

$c = 34$ m $a = 15$ in.

$c = 11.3$ ft. $b = 7$ mi.

$a = 11.4$ cm $c = 22.2$ mm

PAGE 169

3.8 miles

11.6 feet

10.6 centimeters

52.3 inches

PAGE 170

c^2

$\frac{1}{2}ab$

$2ab + c^2$

PAGE 171

a^2

b^2

ab

$2ab + a^2 + b^2$

$c^2 = a^2 + b^2$

PAGE 172

Yes   No

No   No

       Yes

PAGE 173

Yes	Yes
No	No
No	Yes
Yes	No

PAGE 174

Right	Acute
Obtuse	Obtuse
Right	Acute

PAGE 175

5 units	13 units

PAGE 176

2.8 units	6.7 units
8.9 units	6.4 units

PAGE 177

5.4 units	6.7 units
12.7 units	13.6 units

PAGE 178

Answers may vary. All answers are given using 3.14 as an approximation for π.

226.08 in.³	2,289.06 m³
1,570 ft.³	1,846.32 yd.³

PAGE 179

Answers may vary. All answers are given using 3.14 as an approximation for π.

10,597.5 mm³	351.68 cm³
2,260.8 ft.³	7,234.56 m³
14,858.48 yd.³	14,519.36 in.³

PAGE 180

Answers may vary. All answers are given using 3.14 as an approximation for π.

359.01 yd.³	33.49 m³
287.83 in.³	423.9 mm³

PAGE 181

Answers may vary. All answers are given using 3.14 as an approximation for π.

837.33 cm³	65.94 ft.³
452.16 m³	2,051.47 mm³
1,205.76 yd.³	523.33 in.³

PAGE 182

Answers may vary. All answers are given using 3.14 as an approximation for π.

33.49 m³	1,436.03 ft.³
3,052.08 cm³	267.95 yd.³

PAGE 183

Answers may vary. All answers are given using 3.14 as an approximation for π.

2,143.57 m³	4,186.67 in.³
7,234.56 mm³	904.32 ft.³
11,488.21 yd.³	33,493.33 cm³

PAGE 184

Answers may vary. All answers are given using 3.14 as an approximation for π.

4 feet

10 millimeters

7 inches

3 centimeters

PAGE 185

Answers may vary. All answers are given using 3.14 as an approximation for π.

75.36 cubic feet

167.47 cubic centimeters

113.04 cubic inches

523.33 cubic inches

PAGE 187

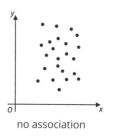

positive association

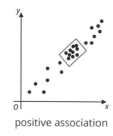

no association

PAGE 187, *continued*

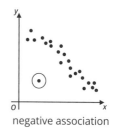

negative association

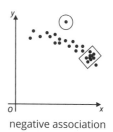

negative association

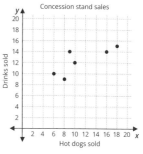

no association

PAGE 188

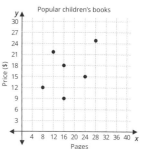

PAGE 189

Scatter plots will vary. Some possible scatter plots are shown below.

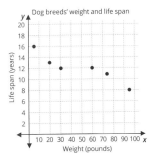

Dog breeds' weight and life span

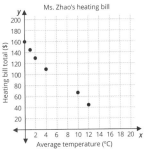

Ms. Zhao's heating bill

PAGE 190

Lines of best fit will vary. Some possible lines of best fit are shown below.

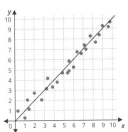

strong positive association

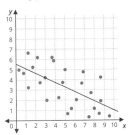

weak negative association

PAGE 191

Lines of best fit will vary. Some possible lines of best fit are shown below.

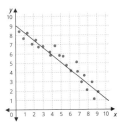

strong negative association

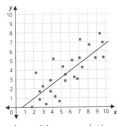

weak positive association

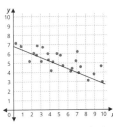

weak negative association

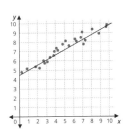

strong positive association

PAGE 192

$y = -\frac{3}{2}x + 19$

Slope = $-\frac{3}{2}$ y-intercept = 19

Explanations may vary. Some possible explanations are shown below.

The slope means that you could expect Luca to drink approximately 1.5 cans of sparkling water each day.

The y-intercept means that you could expect there to be about 19 cans of sparkling water on the day Luca's dad goes shopping.

PAGE 192, *continued*

$y = 10x + 80$

Slope = 10   y-intercept = 80

Explanations may vary. Some possible explanations are shown below.

The slope means that you could expect Mr. Bryant to sell about 10 more ice cream cones for each additional sunny day in a week.

The y-intercept means that you could expect about 80 ice cream cones to be sold in a week with no sunny days.

PAGE 193

$y = \frac{7}{4}x + 3$

17 inches long

12 months old

$y = -4x + 32$

12 ounces

7 kilometers

PAGE 194

	Student	Adult	Total
Friday	38	55	93
Saturday	32	73	105
Total	70	128	198

PAGE 195

	Water	Juice	Total
Salad	36	28	64
Sandwich	22	43	65
Total	58	71	129

	Marinara	Pesto	Total
Penne	14	6	20
Angel hair	31	26	57
Total	45	32	77

PAGE 195, *continued*

	Food	No food	Total
Arcade	72	15	87
No arcade	49	28	77
Total	121	43	164

PAGE 196

Seventh grade

True

$\dfrac{1}{5}$

Children's haircut

False

$\dfrac{1}{4}$

PAGE 197

Grilled cheese

True

$\dfrac{2}{21}$

Annual pass

True

$\dfrac{13}{76}$

PAGE 199

	16-inch	20-inch	Total
Gold	25%	15%	40%
Silver	45%	15%	60%
Total	70%	30%	100%

	Dog park	Skate park	Total
East side	32%	20%	52%
West side	36%	12%	48%
Total	68%	32%	100%

PAGE 200

20%

True

56%

21%

False

Country of Mystery

PAGE 201

Digital poster

Paper poster

Paper poster

Adult

True

Climbing wall

PAGE 202

$p = 14$	$b = 70$	$k = 10$
$r = -6$	$n = -21$	$d = 7.5$
$a = -10$	$v = 8$	$t = -\dfrac{1}{7}$

PAGE 203

(2, 18)	(–3, –3)
(8, 7)	(10, –10)
(2, –1)	(–5, 3)

PAGE 204

Function	Not a function	Function
Brownies: $9.72		Muffins: $15.56
Brownies: $16.20		Muffins: $20.60

PAGE 205

$125

$y = 125x$

$110

$95

$y = 110x + 95$

Explanations will vary. One possible explanation is shown below.

Ordering from Band Essentials would cost $1,875. Ordering from Uniform Utopia would cost $1,745. If they want to choose the cheaper option, they should order from Uniform Utopia.

PAGE 206

Layouts will vary. One possible layout is shown below.

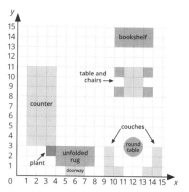

Answers will vary. Some possible answers are shown below.

The table and chairs could be mapped from the old location to the new location by a translation 1 unit to the right and 2 units up.

The bookshelf could be mapped from the old location to the new location by a translation 9 units to the right.

PAGE 207

Answers will vary. Some possible answers are shown below.

The couches are congruent because you can map one couch onto the other with a reflection across the line $x = 12$.

The two regions are similar because you can map one region onto the other using a sequence of transformations including a dilation. The region covered by the folded rug can be mapped to the region covered by the unfolded rug by a dilation from the origin by a scale factor of 2 followed by a translation 4 units to the right and 1 unit up.

The plant can be mapped from the old location to the new location with a reflection across the line $y = 7$.